PERSPECTIVES

A Multicultural Portrait of
The Great Depression

By Susan Rensberger

BENCHMARK BOOKS

MARSHALL CAVENDISH
NEW YORK

Cover: During the Great Depression, the administration of President Franklin Delano Roosevelt created many programs designed to put people to work and to stimulate the economy. As a group, these programs, known as the New Deal, helped promote the belief that it was government's responsibility to help assure the economic and social well-being of the American people.

Benchmark Books
Marshall Cavendish Corporation
99 White Plains Road
Tarrytown, New York 10591-9001, U.S.A.

© Marshall Cavendish Corporation, 1996

Edited, designed, and produced by Water Buffalo Books, Milwaukee

All rights reserved. No part of this book may be reproduced or utilized in any form or by any means electronic or mechanical, including photocopying or recording, or by any information storage and retrieval system, without permission from the copyright holders.

Editorial consultant: Richard Taylor, History Department (Adjunct), the University of Wisconsin-Parkside

Picture Credits: © The Bettmann Archive: Cover, 8, 9, 10, 18, 21, 27, 28, 29, 31, 38, 39, 42, 43, 44, 46, 49, 51, 56, 58, 59, 61, 62; © Charles Phelps Cushing/H. Armstrong Roberts: 41, 68; © H. Armstrong Roberts: 75; © UPI/Bettmann: 6, 11 (both), 12, 13, 14, 15, 17, 19, 22, 30, 32, 33, 34, 36, 40, 45, 50, 53, 55, 60, 65, 66, 67, 69, 71, 72.

Library of Congress Cataloging-in-Publication Data

Rensberger, Susan.
    A multicultural portrait of the great depression / by Susan Rensberger.
       p. cm. -- (Perspectives (Marshall Cavendish Corporation))
    Includes bibliographical references and index.
    Summary: Describes the history of the Great Depression from the vantage point of minorities and women.
    ISBN 0-7614-0053-2 (lib. bdg.)
    1. United States--History--1933-1945--Juvenile literature. 2. Depressions--1929--United States--Juvenile literature. 3. Pluralism (Social sciences)--United States--History--20th century--Juvenile literature. 4. Minorities--United States--History--20th century--Juvenile literature. [1. United States--History--1933-1945. 2. Depressions--1929. 3. Minorities--History.] I. Title. II. Series.
    E806.R46   1995
    973.917--dc20
                                                        95-11029
                                                        CIP
                                                          AC

To PS – MS

Printed in Malaysia
Bound in the U.S.A.

CONTENTS

Introduction 4

Chapter One: Mirrors of Life:
Hard Times Reflected in Art and Culture 6
Radio Entertainment at Home • Messages of Hatred and Hope • Movies Reflect Life in the Thirties • Segregation in the Movies • Race Films • Music, from Classical to Swing • National Art Under the New Deal • Artists on Their Own • A Turning Point for America

Chapter Two: It All Came Tumbling Down: The Politics of Disaster ..22
A Boom Built on Risky Investments • The Downward Slide • From Boom to Bust • From Wall Street to Main Street • From Trust to Fear • The Depression Reshapes Society • New Political Alliances • For Some, a Deeper Depression • Growing Up Early

Chapter Three: Family Roles:
Men and Women Face the Depression 34
Women Working Outside the Home • Added Worries, Added Work • Losing Face: Men in the Depression • Living Simply, Spending Little

Chapter Four: Growing Up Fast: Children in the Great Depression ...46
Taking to the Road • School: A Safe, Warm Place • After Childhood – What Next? • Betty Coed and Joe College • Children on the Road

Chapter Five: Working in the Great Depression 56
Working in Rural America • No Land of Their Own: Tenant Farmers • The Dust Bowl • The Plight of Immigrant Farm Workers • The Indian New Deal • Work in Cities and Towns • Discrimination Against African-Americans and Women • Boycotts and Rioting in Harlem • Working in the Factories • Workers Rebel • The End of the Depression

Chronology, Glossary, Further Reading 76

Index 79

INTRODUCTION

About *Perspectives*

Perspectives is a series of multicultural portraits of events and topics in U.S. history. Each volume examines these events and topics not only from the perspective of the white European-Americans who make up the majority of the U.S. population, but also from that of the nation's many people of color and other ethnic minorities, such as African-Americans, Asian-Americans, Hispanic-Americans, and American Indians. These people, along with women, have been given little attention in traditional accounts of U.S. history. And yet their impact on historical events has been great.

The terms *American Indian, Native American, Hispanic-American, Latino, Anglo-American, Black, African-American,* and *Asian-American*, like *European-American* and *white*, are used by the authors in this series to identify people of various national origins. Labeling people is a serious business, and what we call a group depends on many things. For example, a few decades ago it was considered acceptable to use the words *colored* or *Negro* to label people of African origin. Today, these words are outdated and often a sign of ignorance or outright prejudice. Some even consider *Black* less acceptable than *African-American* because it focuses on a person's skin color rather than national origins. And yet *Black* has many practical uses, especially to describe people whose origins are not only African but Caribbean or Latin American as well.

If we must label people, it's better to be as specific as possible. That is a goal of *Perspectives* — to be as precise and fair as possible in the labeling of people by race, ethnicity, national origin, or other factors, such as gender, sexual orientation, or disability. When necessary and possible, Americans of Mexican origin will be called *Mexican-Americans*. Americans of Irish origin will be called *Irish-Americans*, and so on. The same goes for American Indians: When possible, specific Indians are identified by their tribal names, such as the Winnebago or *Mohawk*. But in a discussion of various Indian groups, tribal origins may not always be entirely clear, and so it may be more practical to use *American Indian*, a term that has widespread use among Indians and non-Indians alike.

Even within a group, individuals may disagree over the labels they prefer for their group: *Black* or *African-American*? *Hispanic* or *Latino*? *American Indian* or *Native American*? *White, Anglo,* or *European-American*? Different situations often call for different labels. The labels used in *Perspectives* represent an attempt to be fair, accurate, and perhaps most importantly, to be mindful of what people choose to call *themselves*.

A Note About *The Great Depression*

When people think about the most important points in history, the events that change the way people live and countries are governed, they often think first of wars. But some of the most important battles in the life of a nation and its people are the ones fought simply to survive, to have food and shelter and clothes to wear.

The Great Depression of the 1930s was an event that changed both the way Americans lived and the way our nation is governed. It occurred between the two great wars of this century, World Wars I and II, yet it made as many changes is this country as those wars did around the world.

The Great Depression was a time when so many people were out of work, and those who had jobs made so little money, that people who had never been poor before faced hunger, cold, and fear. Those who had always been poor lost what little they had, and many were forced to wander the roads and the rails, looking for work or food. Some families were drawn together by the challenges of the Great Depression, but fear and desperation and the need to work tore apart many others.

For many, particularly those who had already faced the rigors of unemployment, discrimination, and prejudice both in their neighborhoods and in the workplace, the Great Depression offered not so much a major change in situation as a new vantage point from which they could view their lives. For many struggling or impoverished African-Americans, Latinos, Asian-Americans, American Indians, and European-Americans, the Great Depression merely lessened their already-slim chances for prosperity. Now, it seemed, the playing field may have leveled off somewhat, but not necessarily in their favor; there were simply more people jostling one another for a smaller share of riches.

Laid off from work and forced out of their homes, Americans began to question how much each person is responsible for taking care of himself or herself and what responsibility we share for the welfare of each other. Those questions are still debated today, more than half a century later.

The Great Depression was also a period when people sought work — and were put to work — in new and imaginative ways. The government created opportunities for employment — from constructing buildings and highways to writing and painting — that allowed people to use their talents even as they helped rebuild a crumbling economy.

The Great Depression was a time of turmoil and drama. You can sense it in the stories of your grandparents. You can hear and see its impact in some of the art, music, literature, cinema, and drama that are taken for granted today. You experience the legacy of the Great Depression when you eat a school lunch because this program started during the Depression. The effects of this important point in our history are all around us — even today — if you know where to look.

Ivie Anderson, a prominent jazz vocalist of the 1930s, with legendary bandleader Duke Ellington. For decades, female vocalists had a much easier time finding work than did women who played musical instruments.

CHAPTER ONE

Mirrors of Life: Hard Times Reflected in Art and Culture

The Great Depression was a time of turmoil for most Americans, a time when the jobs and homes they thought they could count on suddenly were gone — or could be lost at any moment. Getting food, clothing, and a bed to sleep in became an everyday struggle for many, and a drawn-out decade of grim news and endless worry gave people a craving for anything to entertain themselves. The new technology of radio was becoming a staple of American life; games like miniature golf and bridge distracted millions of players; and with television still a few years off, movies enjoyed their golden age during the Great Depression.

Our most enduring images of life during the Great Depression, which started in 1929 and did not end until the United States entered World War II in 1941, are found in the arts and popular culture of the time. In old radio programs, movies, songs, recordings, books, paintings, and photographs, we see the varied faces of Depression America: the thin and desperate faces of the hungry and homeless, the "race" movies produced for segregated Black audiences, the speeches of the first president to use broadcasting as a means of speaking directly to U.S. voters, and novels about the fight for survival of poor tenant farmers evicted from their homes.

Realistic works about American subjects were popular in every art form as Americans became absorbed in their own problems. Writers, painters, musicians, and other artists tried to create work that would inspire social change rather than simply be beautiful or entertaining. As "social relevance" became important in art, the rich and powerful lost their starring roles, and ordinary people became the new heroes.

The arts of the 1930s — including novels, painting, plays, and photography — showed in realistic terms the pain of the unemployed, the homeless, and the powerless. Popular culture, meanwhile — from radio serials and movies, show tunes and dance music, to religious revivals — tried to inspire the hope,

Franklin Delano Roosevelt

Although he was wealthy his whole life, President Franklin D. Roosevelt managed to make people think of him as a champion of ordinary people. As a result of his success, he served longer than any other U.S. president, from 1933 to his death in April 1945 while still in office. He was elected four times and led the nation through the Great Depression and most of World War II. He and his wife, Eleanor, became symbols of their era.

FDR was born in Hyde Park, New York, and was a distant cousin of President Theodore Roosevelt. In 1905, he married Teddy Roosevelt's niece, Anna Eleanor Roosevelt, who as First Lady became as well known as and possibly more popular than her husband. Franklin Roosevelt was elected to the New York State Senate and appointed assistant secretary of the navy by President Woodrow Wilson. He ran for vice president in 1920, but the Democrats lost.

A year later, FDR contracted polio, which left him paralyzed from the waist down. At that time, the public believed disabled people were not healthy enough to do hard work, so FDR took care to hide his paralysis. He made it appear that he had overcome the illness through sheer will, though in fact he often had to be carried by aides and had many special devices built to help him move about freely using his wheelchair. Reporters did not write about Roosevelt's paralysis, just as they did not write about other aspects of the private lives of political leaders. At that time, the press only covered politicians' public statements and actions, believing that their private lives did not affect their qualifications for office. Today, with the press and popular media generating an enormous interest in the life of virtually any public figure, it is clear that times have indeed changed.

FDR was the first and only president to run for more than two terms. After his death, Congress passed a law limiting the presidency to two terms, and so no one else has had as long a period of influence and power as Franklin Roosevelt. Most historians agree that no other politician of the twentieth century has played as important a role in U.S. history as Franklin D. Roosevelt.

endurance, strength, faith, and generosity that were necessary for survival.

During the Great Depression, as jobs became scarce and competition for them fierce, the tendency to blame others for life's troubles grew stronger and more visible in U.S. society. The poorest groups with the least social status — minorities and immigrants — were the most often blamed, though they also suffered more poverty. Lynchings of African-Americans in the South rose; racist white people believed that Blacks had no right to jobs if whites needed work; Filipino farm workers on the West Coast were violently attacked; and Mexican immigrants and Mexican-American farm workers were deported.

Some survivors of the Depression remember it as a time of pulling together, sharing, caring for family and neighbors, and learning that you can overcome almost anything with the help of fellow human beings. One African-American man who grew up in a small midwestern town remembers that his house was the first place hoboes stopped when they got off a train. "We never turned anyone away hungry," he said. "It might not have been much, but my mother always had something for them."

But others remember a time when those who had enough money looked down on those who did not, and those who had little looked for somebody to blame. A woman who spent her Depression childhood in Pittsburgh recalls the little girl across the street who ate candy on her front stoop where neighbor children who could not afford any treats could see her. Still other Americans, looking for someone to blame for their suffering, chose people they knew little or nothing about to make the enemy.

In American culture of the 1930s, we see reflections of all these responses to a nation's hard times.

Radio: Entertainment at Home

The most lasting symbol of life in the thirties may be the radio. Although not every family could afford a radio, most middle-class and working-class people could, and the radio became a central feature of family life. By 1933, half the population of the United States owned radios — more than sixteen million American families. Radios brought entertainment, companionship, information, advice, and comfort to people who needed encouragement.

With the relatively new radio networks, people all across the country could listen to the same programs. Advertisers, politicians, and preachers were just discovering the efficiency of radio broadcasting for selling their products and ideas, and people tended to believe what they heard.

Radio played an important part in the 1932 presidential election, much as television would three decades later. President Herbert Hoover, whom most Americans blamed for not acting to help victims of the Depression, was uncomfortable speaking on radio. His challenger for the presidency, Franklin D. Roosevelt, used his talent for speaking naturally and convincingly to win the election.

Throughout his presidency, which lasted four terms, President Roosevelt used the radio to speak to Americans as no previous president had — personally, in their homes. He made people feel he was trying to help them, even when government programs failed to make their lives better. Almost one-third of the American radio audience heard his very first "fireside chat," broadcast only a few days after he took office.

An Iowa farmer reads a newspaper in front of his radio. Like television today, the radio in the 1930s provided many Americans with an affordable, relaxing form of entertainment.

Down to His Last Possession

People applying for government help in the 1930s had to prove they owned nothing they could sell to pay the rent or buy food. One man pleaded, "All we've got left is a radio. Can't we even hang onto that?"

Mirrors of Life

Freeman Gosden and Charles Correll, in blackface as "Amos 'n' Andy." Though one of the most popular radio comedies of the 1930s, the show reinforced negative stereotypes about African-Americans of the day.

Women listened to the radio to get recipes and learn new ways of stretching the household budget. Families gathered around the radio in the evening to hear weekly dramatic or comedy series. "Amos 'n' Andy," in which two white men played two Black men, reinforcing virtually every negative stereotype about African-Americans of the day, was one of the most popular radio comedies of the era.

Messages of Hatred and Hope

Religious programs became popular in the thirties, as people facing uncertainty and hardship sought hope, strength, and comfort in religious faith. Some Christian evangelists traveled the countryside, finding new audiences for revival meetings held in tents and churches. But other preachers found they could reach many more souls through the new medium of radio.

Father Charles Coughlin, called the Radio Priest, had the largest radio audience in the world. Some thirty to forty million people tuned in to hear his messages blending religion, politics, and anti-Semitism (racism against Jews). In his early years, he blamed the Depression on the concentration of wealth in too few hands and said social justice depended on distributing wealth more equally. He supported Franklin Roosevelt when he was first elected president in 1932.

Records Hit Hard Times

Radio offered free entertainment when millions of people were short of cash. As a result, record sales dropped from more than one hundred million dollars in 1927 to six million dollars in 1933. Many smaller recording companies went out of business, major labels cut the price of records by more than half, and musicians had an even harder time than usual finding a job. African-Americans in particular, whose blues, jazz, and gospel recordings had become popular in the 1920s with both Black and white audiences, suffered as record companies closed their divisions devoted to African-American music, and smaller record companies that sold primarily Black music went bankrupt.

Reverend Charles E. Coughlin, the "Radio Priest," used the radio to spread his message of hatred toward Jews, African-Americans, and others. Eventually, his message became too extreme even for many of his 30-40 million listeners, then the largest radio audience in the world.

Virginia Payne, as the fictional character "Ma Perkins," offered optimism to American listeners who were eager to believe that life would get better. One of the most lasting radio personalities, she reached millions of listeners from 1933 to 1960.

As the decade wore on, though, the Radio Priest became more enthralled with his own power and favored foreign dictators like Adolf Hitler and Benito Mussolini. These men were rising to power in Germany and Italy with messages based on blaming minorities, notably Jews, for the economic woes of the ethnic majority. Their solution was to hold absolute power themselves and destroy anyone they considered an enemy. Their philosophy was called fascism, and it fostered hatred, suspicion, and blame among ethnic groups. It also led to the slaughter of millions of Jews, Poles, Gypsies, and other ethnic and religious minorities, as well as Socialists, Communists, homosexuals, disabled people, and many intellectual and religious leaders. Father Coughlin eventually lost his popularity when his message became one of hatred and racism and his identification with Fascist and Nazi ideology became too blatant to ignore. But many Americans in the thirties, like today, found it easier to blame their fears and problems on people they could imagine as cartoon-character villains than on invisible economic forces they could not understand.

Radio in the 1930s was a powerful medium for spreading hope as well as hatred, and the most lasting radio personalities were those who offered optimism to Americans eager to believe life would get better. One 1930s fictional radio character whose popularity lasted long beyond the decade was Ma Perkins, a widow running a lumber business and raising a family after her husband's death. Ma Perkins's show was broadcast daily at lunchtime on two radio networks and many independent stations, reaching

Mirrors of Life

Playing to Keep Fear Away

Even during the Depression — or maybe especially then, when everyday life could be so grim — people who were working spent money playing. For many people, the Depression meant more fear and worry than deep poverty, and games like miniature golf and contract bridge offered a distraction. Americans spent ten million dollars on bridge lessons in 1931 alone, and the game became a popular way for friends and neighbors to entertain themselves cheaply at home.

Miniature golf was invented in 1930, and for one year it swept the country. Courses were set up everywhere, not just outdoors but in converted theaters and office buildings in major cities. Workers played on their lunch hour. Families took Sunday drives to play on suburban courses. One course in Hollywood featured a live bear chained at one hole. In that one year, Americans spent millions of dollars playing miniature golf, even as unemployment rose and wages fell. But the craze was short-lived, and by the following year, America's attention had turned to other subjects.

millions of listeners from 1933 to 1960. Virginia Payne, the actress who played the part of Ma, described her character's appeal: "She represented what a great many women were doing, and she lived their experiences. She also believed in prayer. You see, it wasn't a cynical age. They had to hope, they had to believe. Ma was one of them."

Movies Reflect Life in the Thirties

Next to radio, movies were probably the most influential form of popular culture in the thirties. They were cheap, even for the time; a ticket cost between a dime and a quarter. There were many more movie theaters than today, and more movies were produced to feed the fierce appetite of Americans for the big screen. Theaters competed for audiences and sometimes gave away gifts such as inexpensive glassware, dishes, and toys to attract moviegoers. Americans bought 60-75 million movie tickets every week, a number equalling more than 60 percent of the nation's population. Though many of those tickets were sold to repeat customers, this still means that more people went to the movies than would be true after television had become established in U.S. homes. By the late 1970s, the number of movie tickets sold weekly equalled less than 10 percent of the population.

Hollywood's movies provided escape for daily problems, of course, but they also may have given people a way to think about those problems and make sense of them. Early in the Depression years, fugitive and gangster films became popular. These movies expressed the hopelessness of people victimized by life. Sometimes the gangster was the victim, a person whose life was so difficult he had been reduced to becoming an outlaw to survive, though he kept some good qualities, such as loyalty and an ability to love. In other movies, the gangster was a symbol of greed and heartlessness, like the bankers and businessmen whom victims of the Depression blamed for their suffering.

By the mid-thirties, musicals were becoming a popular form of escape from grinding daily worries. These movies featured huge production numbers with many dancers in elaborate costumes and songs with titles like "We're in the Money." Individual performers like Ginger Rogers and Fred Astaire, dancing their way to love and happiness, became popular, too.

Adult performers were not the only ones helping Depression audiences escape the hopelessness of everyday life. Everyone loved Hollywood's version of childhood — plucky child stars like Shirley Temple or Spanky, Alfalfa, Buckwheat, and other members of The Little Rascals facing problems and solving them with courage and little help from the adult world.

Social relevance swept the movies, too, as it did other art forms. Late in the decade, directors like John Ford and Frank Capra made movies about human values and social justice. Capra's movies, such as *Mr. Smith Goes to Washington* and *Mr. Deeds Goes to Town*, associated rural and small-town life with honesty, fairness, and generosity, while urban culture was equated with cynicism and selfishness.

Such John Ford movies as *The Grapes of Wrath*, the 1940 film version of John Steinbeck's story about farmers made homeless by the Dust Bowl, and *How Green Was My Valley*, the 1941 movie about miners fighting the power of mine owners, dealt directly with Depression-era themes. Moviegoers had the opportunity to see their problems reflected on the screen and put in the context of larger social movements.

Roles for women in movies varied from the anonymous chorus-line dancer whose body became an abstract object, to the strong, independent leading roles played by Katherine Hepburn, Rosalind Russell, Bette Davis, and Joan Craw-

Child performers like Shirley Temple, shown here with Bill "Bojangles" Robinson, helped Depression audiences escape everyday life. White children were often portrayed as more mature and intelligent than Black characters in the same movies.

Mirrors of Life

ford. Early in the decade, women in some films pursued sexual relationships with men. While sex wasn't shown on screen, the dialogue strongly suggested that it took place off screen. Mae West, whose movie dialogue was peppered with wisecracks and suggestive double meanings, was known for her portrayals of aggressive, sexually forward vamps. She also earned the nation's second-highest income in 1935: $480,833.

By the mid-thirties, an outcry led by an organization called the National League for Decency demanded the film industry be cleaned up. Hollywood responded in 1934 by setting up a system of self-regulation before Congress could get around to imposing one of its own.

While it limited women's roles as sexual equals with men, the Production Code also prompted new roles to be designed for them. Battle-of-the-sexes films became popular, in which women pursued careers and men pursued them. The women in these films were smart, tough equals to their male counterparts, and the emphasis was on witty dialogue. In the end, however, these films never really challenged traditional roles or power in relationships. As they battled, the man learned new respect for the woman, who then decided to give up everything they had been fighting for to marry him. His power increased when she gave up hers. These movies left unchallenged the assumption that women had to choose between a career and a family and that even smart, capable women ultimately found marriage more fulfilling than careers.

Mae West, known for her suggestive, witty dialogue and heavily made-up portrayals of aggressive, sexually forward vamps, earned the nation's second-highest income in 1935, at $480,833.

Segregation in the Movies

The United States in the 1930s was still a segregated nation, whether by law in the South or custom in the North. Segregation in public accommodations, such as restaurants, theaters, and hotels, was legal. The entertainment industry was as segregated as the rest of society. Not only were theaters segregated, catering to either whites or African-Americans, but not both, but movie companies actually produced one kind of movie for white audiences and another for "colored" (the most common term of the day for African-Americans).

After the box-office failure of *Hearts in Dixie* and *Hallelujah* — two widely discussed movies in the late 1920s that attempted to portray African-Americans as strong, interesting characters in their own right — Hollywood spent the 1930s making movies for white audiences that reinforced their stereotypes about African-Americans. Black characters never questioned or complained about their place in society. Men generally played butlers, train porters, and chauffeurs. Black women played maids and nannies. They spoke in dialect and were often portrayed as foolish, superstitious, and childlike. Even white children such as Shirley Temple, who enjoyed enormous popularity in the thirties, were shown as more mature and intelligent than Black characters in the same movies.

African-American patrons line up at a segregated Memphis theater in 1937 featuring a "short" subject of boxer Joe Louis. Movie companies produced one kind of movie for white audiences and another for "colored" people.

Despite the dismal roles they were offered, some African-American actors and actresses managed to become well-known stars and steal scenes from their white counterparts. One of the best known was a performer named Stepin Fetchit. He played some of the most degrading roles as a foolish flunky, but he played them with flawless comic timing. When he occasionally appeared in a film made for Black moviegoers, his clownish character was accepted by audiences as just one among many images of African-Americans. In white-cast movies, though, that same character played into stereotypically racist images of Black men in general.

Other prominent African-American actors of the thirties included Eddie "Rochester" Anderson, who shared the screen with famous comedians such as W. C. Fields and, later, Jack Benny. Anderson often played a self-confident servant who could manipulate his employer to get what he wanted. Bill "Bojangles" Robinson became famous for his dancing in such Shirley Temple movies as The Little Colonel.

Paul Robeson was a powerful African-American actor with a strength that no role could disguise. He opened his commercial movie career in 1933 with the lead role in The Emperor Jones, based on a play by Eugene O'Neill. He had already played the role on Broadway and London, and the film version became a classic. Throughout his career, Robeson tried to find strong dramatic roles. For the most part, he had to look beyond Hollywood to independent film makers in the United States and to British producers. Robeson eventually moved to England, where he found less racial discrimination than in the United States.

African-American actress Hattie McDaniel, working with stereotypical servant roles, used her tone of voice to make it clear she had little patience for the white people for whom she worked. Her best-remembered role was as Mammy in the 1939 classic, Gone with the Wind. Though the film showed African-Americans as loyal slaves with no concern beyond their owners' welfare, Hattie McDaniel gave a strong performance as the servant who was not afraid to tell Scarlett O'Hara what she thought of her manipulations. McDaniel won the Academy Award for Best Supporting Actress for her performance — the first African-American to win an Oscar.

Another African-American actress successful in Hollywood was Louise Beavers, who starred in the 1934 movie *Imitation of Life*. The movie depicts a friendship between two women — one European-American, the other African-American — that, though supposedly close, keeps racial class distinctions intact. The white woman exploits the Black woman, who refuses to accept any ownership in their shared business and willingly accepts a role in her friend's life barely above servanthood. In a subplot, the Black woman's light-skinned daughter decides to leave home and pretend to be white in order to find a life that is better than her mother's. While white audiences saw a story of interracial friendship that left them unchallenged in their ideas about race and class, African-Americans saw a film that exposed, perhaps unintentionally, the exploitation and racism in American society.

Race Films

Many more African-American performers found acting opportunities outside Hollywood in films made by smaller production companies that catered to the African-American audience. These films were called "race" films, because, to African-Americans in the urban North, the word "race" represented Black pride, and they preferred it over "colored" or "Negro." Because they were made on low budgets, race films were often made quickly, without the best equipment or the technical expertise of Hollywood. Their quality was uneven and generally poorer than that of Hollywood films. But they had one big advantage — they depicted African-Americans as real people.

Some race films addressed social themes such as racism in the United States and divisions within the African-American community, where skin color also could determine a person's status. But many of the most popular were simply Black-cast versions of popular white movie genres — detective stories, gangster movies, and adventure films. Race movies were usually advertised as having "an all-colored cast" and were shown in African-American movie theaters.

One of the most successful African-American filmmakers was Oscar Micheaux. Between 1918 and 1948, he wrote, directed, and produced an estimated thirty to forty films and made his leading actors and actresses into stars. His advertisements compared them to such white stars as Rudolph Valentino and Mae West, using Hollywood's film idols to promote his own pictures. One criticism of his movies was that they featured light-skinned African-Americans and helped reinforce the attitude that Black society should imitate the white society around it.

Music, from Classical to Swing

Another popular pastime in the 1930s was listening and dancing to live music. Big bands were popular, and dancers crowded the floor to move to the new sound called swing, a style derived from the jazz that had been so popular in the twenties. Dance orchestras toured the country, packing in big crowds even in small cities.

Female musicians had a hard time getting jobs during the thirties because, although many popular orchestras featured female vocalists, few orchestras took women seriously as musicians playing instruments. This was true from symphony orchestras to Hollywood studio orchestras to swing bands. Women musicians could get jobs in movies pretending to play musical instruments, but they were shut out from the higher-paid orchestras that actually recorded the sound track. One way women found work was to form "all-girl" dance orchestras, which were very popular during the Depression.

In classical music, women had an even harder time. Harpists were the only women musicians who could readily get work with a major orchestra; many hired no women at all. In 1936, only eight women's orchestras existed, employing a meager total of 522 classical musicians. Some had existed for decades, such as the Los Angeles Women's Symphony, but others in Chicago, Boston, and New York were started during the thirties. Opportunities for minority musicians were even scarcer. But in 1933, Florence Price became the first African-American woman composer to have a piece performed by a major American orchestra, the Chicago Symphony.

Like the rest of society, the popular music industry was segregated in the 1930s. During the twenties, Americans had started listening to African-American musicians playing blues, jazz, and gospel music sold on "race" records. As with movies, race records were mostly produced by small, independent companies devoted to recording African-American music and marketing it to both Black and white audiences. Some of the large record companies, seeing the success of race records, opened separate "race" divisions. But the onset of the Depression caused the bottom to drop out of the recording industry, and most independent producers folded.

Edward Kennedy "Duke" Ellington, seated at the piano with his band. With other African-American musicians, artists, and writers of the 1920s and 1930s, he led a lively movement known as the Harlem Renaissance.

Mirrors of Life

Swing, the most popular music in the thirties, was developed from traditional jazz by African-American musicians, led by bandleader Fletcher Henderson and arranger Don Redman. They adapted jazz to the larger bands that were popular in nightclubs. The most famous African-American swing bandleaders of the Depression era were Duke Ellington at the Cotton Club in Harlem, where Black artists played for white customers, and Count Basie, whose band in Kansas City developed a more bluesy swing that showed rural influences.

African-American vocalists found their recording opportunities disappearing with the Depression, but they continued to be popular with audiences around the country. Jazz and blues artists included Fats Waller, Louis Armstrong, Billie Holiday, and Ella Fitzgerald. Mahalia Jackson was a prominent female gospel singer of the period, and African-American vocal quartets became popular, including the Mills Brothers and the Ink Spots.

National Art Under the New Deal

Today, few people working in the arts — which include literature, painting, sculpture, photography, theater, music, and dance — make enough money to live on from practicing their art. But for a time in the 1930s, things were different. Along with other types of work relief provided by the New Deal — the name given to FDR's plan to promote economic recovery and social reform — were programs that hired writers, musicians, artists, playwrights, and actors to create "art for the millions." Government projects brought classical music, theater, and public works of art to people who had not had much opportunity to enjoy them before.

At the same time, the projects provided work for artists at a time when it was hard to sell books, paintings, and tickets to concerts or plays. By putting artists to work just as engineers and architects were employed building bridges and hospitals, the government did something else for the arts: It said that art, music, writing, and acting are important to society.

Federal Writers Project. The Federal Writers Project (FWP) employed five thousand creative writers, researchers, and administrators and produced one thousand publications. Its most famous books are state guides that included history, folklore, and sightseeing information; they were so good that they are still used today. Another project collected ethnic folklore and the stories of former slaves. The program hired writers regardless of race or ethnic background. Such famous writers as Richard Wright, Ralph Ellison, Saul Bellow, John Cheever, Margaret Walker, Tillie Olsen, and Zora Neale Hurston once worked for the FWP.

Richard Wright, author of *Native Son*, along with other famous writers, once worked for the Federal Writers Project, a program that hired writers regardless of race or ethnic background.

In the early years of the project, writers were paid to do creative work. But later, the public and Congress began to question the "usefulness" of creative writing, and administrators assigned fiction writers to work on guidebooks and other nonfiction projects. In its later years, the FWP was a hard employer, demanding a certain number of words every day from its writers. Anyone who did not meet the quota had to turn in twice as many the next day. Writers became disillusioned with the project and its production-line approach to a creative process.

Federal Art Project. The goal of the Federal Art Project was "art for the millions," and although critics disagreed on the quality of art produced, the project did succeed in making art a more visible part of U.S. life. The project created twenty-five hundred murals in public buildings, seventeen thousand sculptures, and thousands of other works of art. Two million people visited the project's art exhibit at the 1940 New York World's Fair. The project also ran one hundred community art centers around the country and encouraged the practice of Native American crafts. At its peak, the Federal Art Project employed more than two thousand artists, including some such as Jackson Pollack and Willem De Kooning, whose work would later become famous. Female artists were treated more fairly on federal projects than by the art world in general, making up nearly half the number of artists employed.

The Federal Arts Projects had problems with politicians who, responsible for funding the programs, understood little about art. Politicians in the thirties were especially wary of anything that might be interpreted as supporting communism, and some of the public murals that showed the struggles of laborers were criticized for being "un-American."

Federal Theater Project. If political controversy created a problem for visual artists, it was even worse for one of the shortest-lived and most inventive art projects, the Federal Theater Project. From 1935 to 1939, the project produced plays seen by more than twenty-five million Americans. It produced *Macbeth* with an all-Black cast and discussed political issues of the day through pieces the project called "living newspapers."

New ideas, especially those that urged people to question government policies, were not popular with politicians by late in the New Deal. Conservatives were tired of spending money on so many new agencies and programs and were looking for a way to reclaim power from President Roosevelt. The theater project was an easy target because it was visible, tried new ideas, and produced

Cast members of an all-Black swing version of *The Mikado*. The Chicago production was financed by the government until Congress cut off the funding of such theaters in 1939, bringing an end to the production's dream of taking the show to Broadway.

Mirrors of Life 19

plays on subjects relevant to everyday life. Congress decided not to renew its funding in 1939, and, unlike many European governments, the U.S. government has never since supported a national theater.

Federal Music Project. The Federal Music Project had less trouble keeping political support because it concentrated on classical music. The project established orchestras in cities where there had been none, gave free concerts and music lessons, and created orchestras to tour the country. In addition to making classical music more widely available, the project collected and preserved American folk music, much of which would otherwise be lost today.

One shortcoming of the Federal Music Project is that it did not provide the opportunities to women that other federal arts projects did. Only 2,253 of its 15,000 musicians were women, a record not much better than the rest of the male-dominated classical music field of the thirties.

Nor did the efforts of the Federal Music Project survive after the Depression. Few of its orchestras were revived after World War II intervened, and none of the arts projects established a permanent role for the government in supporting the arts.

Artists on Their Own

The Depression had other effects on the arts besides drawing government support. The impulse to document the dramatic problems and exciting social changes of the day, such as workers joining together in labor unions and farmers striking for higher prices, affected all forms of art.

The thirties saw the rise of "radical journalism," whose writers and photographers sought to change social conditions through their work. Some writers worked in many *genres,* or forms, including journalism, fiction, and documentary film. Journalist Martha Gellhorn, one of many hired by the federal government to document the effect of government programs on people's lives, later wrote a novel about what she had discovered, called *The Trouble I've Seen.* Other journalists similarly combined reporting on real events with writing fiction about characters experiencing those events.

Writers and photographers worked together to show the living conditions of this country's poorest people. In 1936, photographer Margaret Bourke-White and novelist Erskine Caldwell published a book about southern sharecropping called *You Have Seen Their Faces.* This was also the year that writer James Agee and photographer Walker Evans spent four weeks in Alabama, living with one of three white sharecropping families whose lives they would document in *Let Us Now Praise Famous Men.* The book, with its bleak photos and descriptions of grinding rural poverty, became one of the best known of the decade.

The move toward social relevance in art gave rise to a kind of fiction called the proletarian novel — stories about working people struggling against powerful bosses for fair wages, decent working conditions, and human dignity. These novels often depicted strikes or efforts to

---

Books That Sold, Even in Hard Times

The need for security and a place to belong was a theme that dominated the best-selling novels of the Depression years. They were *Gone With the Wind* (1936), *God's Little Acre* (1933), *The Good Earth* (1931), and *The Grapes of Wrath* (1939).

People searching for a way out of economic trouble also flocked to self-help books, such as another best-seller, *How to Win Friends and Influence People* (1937). That book sold 750,000 copies its first year in print.

organize labor unions and tried to interest middle-class readers in the needs of poor workers. Many of these novels were written by women, but few are read today. Like most art created to communicate a political message, their relevance — and some would argue the quality of their writing — rarely outlived their times.

Novelists who wrote simply to create good literature have fared better. Pearl Buck published her famous novel, *The Good Earth*, in 1931; in 1939 she won the world's most prestigious literary prize, the Nobel Prize for Literature. Other famous women writers who got their start during the Depression include Katherine Anne Porter, Carson McCullers, and Mary Sarton.

African-American author Zora Neale Hurston was at the peak of her career in the thirties. The themes of her work arose less from the Depression than from the Harlem Renaissance of the 1920s, when Harlem was a lively center of African-American culture. Artists such as Hurston produced works celebrating their African-American lives, culture, and history. During the 1930s, Hurston worked on the Florida Writers Project and published four novels, making her the most published Black woman writer of her time.

In the visual arts, as in other forms, American themes and styles were popular. The paintings of Anna Mary Robertson "Grandma" Moses, a self-taught artist who painted rural life in a simple style, were first exhibited in 1939. Meanwhile, Georgia O'Keefe, already a famous artist, began painting the images of the southwestern United States for which she was later known.

A Turning Point for America

Although the Depression years impoverished millions of people, they also enriched our culture. Popular entertainment such as movies and music seemed to take on new energy, as though to shake off the weariness of daily life. The arts focused suddenly on the pressing problems of ordinary people. We can still glimpse what life was like for those people through the movies, music, photographs, books, and old radio shows they left behind.

The Depression had other lasting effects on society. It changed public attitudes about helping people in need and created a new role for government in filling those needs. A whole generation of Americans, possibly including your grandparents, grew up in poverty or the fear of poverty. The Depression shaped the way they spent and saved money, planned for the future, and ran the nation.

So just what was the Great Depression and what caused it? To understand, we need to look at how our economy works.

A self-taught artist, Anna Mary Robertson "Grandma" Moses, painted rural life in a simple style that achieved great popularity in the United States in the late 1930s. She was widely known and beloved and has become an institution in the art world.

Mirrors of Life   21

Wall Street on October 24, 1929 — "Black Thursday" — the day that prices on the New York Stock Exchange began spiraling downward, throwing the nation's economy — and people's lives — into turmoil.

CHAPTER TWO

It All Came Tumbling Down: The Politics of Disaster

They called it the Crash. On October 24, 1929 — later called Black Thursday — prices on the New York Stock Exchange took a sudden nosedive. The stock-market crash sent the U.S. economy into a tailspin that would last throughout the 1930s. The country would not fully recover until the early 1940s, when it entered World War II.

This economic disaster was called the Great Depression, and it turned lives upside down. Some people lost their savings, and property became worthless because no one had money to buy it. One woman, who was twenty when the stock market crashed, recalled her youth in the 1930s. "All hell broke loose!" she said. Her father's real estate suddenly lost its value because no one could afford to buy it. The week she turned twenty-one, he committed suicide.

"There was no stigma attached to it [suicide] then," she said. "His partner had jumped a week after the market crashed." On the brink of adulthood, this young woman was left to support her entire family: her mother, younger sister, and her aunt, who had been deserted by her husband.

A Boom Built on Risky Investments

The Crash should not have been a surprise. Everything that goes up must come down, even on the stock exchange. For two years, stock prices had been going up steadily, setting new records, only to break them a few months or even weeks later. Common sense and experience would have predicted that eventually people would be unwilling to pay such inflated prices for shares of stock. Earlier in 1929, investors began reaching that point. Prices had been gradually falling since summer, and from the vantage point of history, it is obvious that a major drop was on its way.

Yet in 1929, the vast majority of Americans were surprised by the Crash when it finally came. They had believed the leading bankers and businesspeople of the day, who said repeatedly that there was no end in sight to the ris-

What Are Stocks?

Businesses need money to build or expand factories, buy machinery or office equipment, purchase materials to make a product, and hire workers. To raise that money, they divide ownership of the company among people willing to invest money in return for a share of company profits. The means of dividing ownership is called issuing stock. Shares of stock can be sold privately by the owners themselves to people they know or publicly through a stock exchange. At a stock exchange, stocks are bought and sold by brokers, whose clients, the buyers, pay them for this service.

The most famous stock exchange in this country is the New York Stock Exchange on Wall Street in New York City. Stocks are also traded on other exchanges, including the American Stock Exchange, also in New York, and regional exchanges in cities around the country.

Owners of stock can make money by receiving shares of company profits, called dividends, if the company is making money. Until 1927, stock prices were rising because companies were making profits and investors wanted a share of them. But when stock prices rise rapidly, investors may be able to make more money, and make it more quickly, by selling their shares than by keeping them and accumulating dividends.

Speculation was a favorite form of investment in the 1920s, whether in land or stocks. Speculation means buying something not because you want to keep it but because you believe you will be able to sell it again at a profit — that is, for more money than you paid for it. In the 1920s, people heard many stories, and even read them in popular magazines, about ordinary Americans getting rich by investing in the stock market. Speculators bought stocks, not because the companies issuing them were prosperous and could pay dividends, but because they were such a popular investment that the prices kept rising.

Most speculators were not satisfied to simply sell for a profit and put their money into safer investments. They wanted to sell for the highest price possible, so they held onto their stocks even after prices had started to dip, believing every downturn was only temporary.

ing stock market. Bankers, stockbrokers, and politicians assured investors that the stocks were still selling below their real value. They were still a safe investment for people who wanted to get rich fast, and many did.

The Downward Slide

Then, in September 1929, investors began to lose confidence in the economy. No one knows exactly why. There were some signs that the economy was slowing down — that is, fewer goods were being produced and sold, so less money was changing hands.

At that point, no one could have actually predicted a depression, yet stock-market prices started to drop a little as fewer people wanted to buy. Speculators started to fear losing money and decided it was time to sell their stock while prices were still higher than what they had paid originally. Prices fell more. Suddenly everyone was selling, nobody was buying, and prices plummeted.

What was worse, many people had borrowed money to buy stocks. Brokerage firms (companies that employ brokers to buy and sell stocks for people who want to invest in the stock market) even lent their customers the money to buy the stocks, which is called buying "on margin." In the 1920s, people could buy stocks by paying cash for as little as 10 percent of the stock's value and borrowing the rest.

When prices fell, stocks bought on margin were worth even less than the value of the loan used to buy them. They could not be sold to repay the loan; the owner's only hope of making back the money was to hold onto the stock and hope its price went back up. As prices dropped, brokerage firms demanded that investors either send more cash or sell their stock at its current value and give all the money to the broker. Investors who had no more money left lost all their original investment, and those who did put up more cash soon lost that, too, as prices kept falling.

Black Thursday was only the beginning of the Crash. Some of the big banks in New York City tried to drive prices back up by buying large amounts of stocks when the prices fell, and for a short time they succeeded. But within a few days, prices spiraled downward again. Tuesday, October 29, has been called by economist John Kenneth Galbraith "the most devastating day in the history of the New York stock market." Prices on the stock exchange continued to fall steeply until the middle of November 1929, then gradually but steadily dropped through the middle of 1932.

The Great Depression had begun.

From Boom to Bust

One reason people in 1929 had so much confidence in their ability to get rich was that the United States had just enjoyed ten years of prosperity. World War I had ended in 1918, and the 1920s were boom days. Soldiers coming home went to work, got married, and needed a house and a car and furniture and appliances. Businesses were eager to produce these goods and hired workers to manufacture and build what was needed. Workers in turn spent their wages to buy goods, creating more jobs and prosperity.

Even in the 1920s, the United States was home to both very rich and very poor people. Women and minorities struggled against discrimination, were less educated, and earned less than white men. But even those at the bottom of the ladder had better jobs and more money than ever in the 1920s.

But by 1927, the economic cycle of earning and spending was slowing down. Most young fam-

How Money Circulates Through the Economy

"The economy" is a term often used but seldom defined. The economy of a country is the total amount of goods and services produced and exchanged. Goods and services are what we buy. A television set, for example, is a good, but the programs on it are services. To produce goods and services, you need three things: *land,* or a place to produce them; *labor,* or people to produce them; and *capital,* or the items used in production such as offices, machines, and factories.

Money changes hands continuously as people do business. For example, a person buys land, builds a factory, buys equipment, hires workers, builds televisions, sells them to customers, and uses the money to build more. Every dollar paid by the factory owner for equipment or supplies or to workers is spent, in turn, on buying other goods and services. Money keeps circulating through the economy, from hand to hand like water in an endless stream.

As long as the stream keeps flowing, the economy functions well. There are enough jobs for those who want them, and people earn money to spend, which pays more workers. Money that's saved can be invested in businesses that need more capital, land, or labor to expand production.

But sometimes the flow of money slows down. Businesses stop investing in making more television sets and producing more programs. Businesses and consumers spend less on products like computers or services like car repair. This means less money changing hands, fewer jobs, less income. When many of the nation's resources are not being used, when factories are not producing as much as they could and people are out of work, we call that an economic *recession*. A very bad recession is called a *depression*.

During a depression, many people can be without jobs, food, housing, and clothing. To get out of a recession or depression, the government tries to get money flowing through the economy again. Some people think the best way to do this is for government to spend large amounts of money, either from taxes already collected or by borrowing money. Other people think government should collect less money in taxes and trust people to invest that money in businesses and buy more products, so there will be more jobs.

> **The Law of Supply and Demand**
>
> One of the laws of economics is called the law of supply and demand. It states that the price of a product or service is related to how much of it is available. Supply and demand work together like a see-saw: The higher the supply of a product or service, the lower its price.
>
> If supply goes down compared to the number of people wanting to buy it, the seller can demand a higher price. For example, if a winter freeze destroys much of Florida's citrus crop, the supply of oranges in supermarkets all across the country goes down, and their price goes up.
>
> The same thing happens if the supply stays the same, but more people want to buy. If more people want the latest style in shoes than the producer can make, the shoes would become expensive. This is what drove up stock prices in the 1920s. The number of people wanting to buy increased faster than the number of stocks for sale.
>
> On the other hand, if the supply of a product or service suddenly goes up, its price will fall. If a second shoe company makes a shoe styled just like the one everyone wants, the price will drop because now kids can buy shoes from either company. The sellers will lower their prices, hoping kids will buy from them rather than from their competitor. This is what happened in 1929. Suddenly, many people wanted to sell the shares of stock they owned, but so few people wanted to buy that the value of the stocks fell to the point of being completely worthless.

ilies had built their houses and bought all the appliances, furniture, and cars they needed. As consumers bought less, businesses needed to produce less, so they laid off some of their workers. They also needed fewer supplies, so fewer workers were needed in related industries as well. For instance, as home building dropped off, so did the lumber industry. As fewer cars and washing machines were bought, fewer were built, and steel workers lost their jobs. Some manufacturers cut wages to save production costs and lower the price of their goods, hoping to sell more. But the less money workers earned, the less they had to buy goods from other manufacturers. The economy began to slide into recession, and then depression.

The economic slowdown that followed the 1929 Crash was so severe it is called the Great Depression: twelve long years of hardship and unemployment. Millions of poor people were unable to pay their rent or buy food or clothing, farmers lost their farms, and middle-class people lost their homes. It was the longest, bleakest period of hard times in U.S. history, lasting through the 1930s.

From Wall Street to Main Street

The stock market crash was not the only factor in creating the Great Depression, but it set off a panic that was quickly felt all the way across the country. When the stock market collapsed, investors lost money and had none to invest even in sound businesses. Companies feared that demand for their products would drop because people would be afraid to spend what money they had, so they slowed production, laid off workers, and cut wages and work hours to save money. As a result, workers had less money to buy goods, forcing even more businesses to lose money or go bankrupt.

Panic spreads as confidence in the nation's economy plummets, causing runs on banks like this, as many people try to withdraw their money at the same time.

Banks, which had been sending money to Wall Street to lend to stock investors, lost money when stock prices fell and people could not repay those loans. Some banks began to go out of business. Ordinary people decided they had better get their money out of their bank before it closed, too. The panic spread, causing "runs" on banks as many people tried to withdraw their money all at the same time.

Banks normally do not keep all of their depositors' money on hand; they lend much of it out to other customers, charge them interest, and make a profit using the depositors' money. As long as borrowers repay their loans with interest, there is always money in the bank when depositors come to make withdrawals. But if borrowers cannot repay the bank, and if too many depositors want to withdraw their money all at once, the bank may run out of cash and be forced to close. That is what happened in the Great Depression.

From Trust to Fear

Like the banking system and the stock market, to a great extent the entire economy runs on trust. As long as everyone believes the economy is going well, money keeps changing hands and the economy hums along. But when people and businesses begin to lose confidence in having a steady income and stop spending money, the whole economy suffers. No foolproof way has been found to get the economy going again, though many economists offer theories and suggestions.

Franklin D. Roosevelt was elected president in 1932 by people who hoped he would know how to lead the country out of the Depression. FDR, as he is often called, became famous for his radio speech-

A Bank "Holiday"

When Franklin D. Roosevelt took office in March 1933, he knew he had to do something fast. Just before inauguration day, there were runs on banks in Illinois and New York. Those states declared bank holidays, meaning they closed all banks for a few days so depositors could not withdraw their money and bankrupt the banks.

The first thing FDR did when he took office was declare a four-day national bank holiday to give people time to calm down. In his first fireside chat, he reassured them that the banking system was still reliable. He was so convincing that when banks opened the next morning, more people deposited money than withdrew it.

It All Came Tumbling Down

Franklin Delano Roosevelt (FDR) was famous for his radio speeches, called "fireside chats," to the American public.

es, in which he tried to calm the fears and renew the faith of the American people in their economy. One of the most often-quoted lines from these "fireside chats," as they were called, was "We have nothing to fear but fear itself."

For Americans in the Great Depression, fear was a constant companion. People who grew up in the 1930s tell stories about learning to save and reuse everything, not only because they had so little today, but because they might have even less tomorrow. The habit of saving and the fear of debt was carried by most of those people into adulthood.

The Depression Reshapes Society

The effects of the Great Depression on the United States would be felt for decades to come. The majority of American people would move from believing that individuals were responsible for their own destiny and got what they deserved, to believing that people are responsible for helping each other. The role of government would change from simply keeping order and staying out of the way to ensuring that all Americans had at least the bare necessities of life. Many of the laws and government programs that we take for granted today — Social Security, public assistance programs, child labor laws, federal insurance for bank deposits, minimum wage levels, the forty-hour work week — would grow out of the Great Depression.

New Political Alliances

Politics in the United States changed dramatically during the 1930s, too. African-Americans deserted the Republican Party of Abraham Lincoln for the first time since the Civil War and voted for a Democrat, Franklin

The Government's New Deal

Franklin Roosevelt promised Americans a "new deal for the forgotten man." This promise of a "new deal" caught the public's imagination. All of FDR's programs aimed at ending the Depression, as well as the period of the 1930s when they were enacted, are named for that promise.

Eleanor Roosevelt, Conscience of a Nation

Anna Eleanor Roosevelt was born in 1884 to a family that included her uncle Theodore Roosevelt, who was elected president in 1901. She became a public figure as the wife of President Franklin D. Roosevelt, but she used that position to create a career for herself as a diplomat, writer, and advocate for women, the underprivileged, and human rights.

Following her husband's death in 1945, she was appointed U.S. delegate to the United Nations, a post she held for seven years. She was appointed to the same position in 1961 and held it until her death the following year. Her writings include a memoir, *This I Remember,* as well as other works.

Eleanor Roosevelt, while not officially part of the U.S. government during her husband's presidency, was the most widely known and one of the most outspoken women in the country. She was often criticized by conservatives for expressing strong, liberal opinions and championing society's oppressed. But she was also beloved as the caring, human face of the administration. She is credited with persuading her husband to address the problems of minorities and the poor. She also influenced him to appoint women to high government positions, many never before held by women, and supported women's causes with special White House meetings and conferences.

As First Lady, Eleanor Roosevelt wrote a newspaper column that was carried in papers across the country, and people felt so strongly that she cared personally about them that during the Depression many wrote appeals to her for help. Most writers were women asking for help in feeding or clothing their children. Some asked if she had any old clothes she might be able to send them.

The American people saw Eleanor Roosevelt as their friend, and she is remembered for changing the role of First Lady from one of wife and hostess to serving as an advocate for people with little or no power in her day, including women and African-Americans.

Roosevelt. When the Depression began, Herbert Hoover, a Republican, was president. Because he continued to defend big business over the needs of workers on questions of wages, hours, and other issues, many people shifted to the Democratic Party.

During the Depression, many people — workers, the poor, and even some middle-class people who feared losing their homes or jobs and who deplored the living conditions of the unemployed — began to see themselves as part of a group. When they felt President Roosevelt was not doing enough to help working and poor people, some of these people began supporting more radical leaders. For a time, interest in socialism and even communism began to grow, as radical ideas filtered into the American political discussion.

Roosevelt began to fear he would not be reelected if he did not help the poor and side with workers against the interests of big business. His shift to policies that favored working-class, poor, and minority voters set the standard for the Democratic Party through the 1980s. The identity of the two major political parties established during the Great Depression has remained largely unchanged, despite periods when Democrats have adopted more conservative positions for political reasons.

"Hardluck Town," New York City, in 1932 — a collection of squatters' shacks that drew destitute Americans looking for work in New York. During the Great Depression, people traveled thousands of miles to pursue the chance, however remote, of finding a job.

From Elephant to Mule

African-Americans gained the vote along with their freedom after the Civil War. Most of them supported the Republican Party because it was the party of Abraham Lincoln. But during the Depression, they began to think differently about the Republican Party (whose symbol is an elephant) and the Democrats (represented by a mule).

One southern African-American tenant farmer told a government writer in the 1930s that he used to vote until laws were passed that made it easy for white people to keep Black people from voting. "If I were to vote today, I'd vote for Roosevelt," he said. "I don't care if he is a Democrat, he helps the poor man and the farmer.... Ever since the [Civil] War, the colored folks has looked on the elephant as the animal that helps 'em. But I'm coming to believe that the elephant may be all right in Africa, but the ... [African-American] ... had better stay close to the American mule."

30 *A Multicultural Portrait of the Great Depression*

For Some, a Deeper Depression

The Great Depression was hard on all Americans, but women and minorities had an even harder time. They lived with stereotypes and discrimination, little power, and less money. Some African-Americans said the Great Depression hardly made any difference — that they had lived in a depression all their lives. Others said they managed to get ahead a little when real estate prices fell during the Depression by buying city property they normally could not have afforded.

One man, who had lived his whole life as a tenant on the same farm where his parents had been slaves, said many Black people were going north to find jobs and less discrimination in Chicago or Detroit. He didn't think this was a good idea. They get paid more, he said, but they also spend more for rent. And what would happen if they lost their jobs? "When they is out of work a northern man won't even give 'em a meal," he said. "What's the good of calling you 'mister' if they won't give you work and won't help you when you're hungry?" At least at home, he felt, he would have somewhere to turn for help if disaster struck.

But for many tenant farmers, there was no such security. For those already dirt poor — especially those living in rural areas and working on land they did not own — the Depression meant losing their tentative hold on stability. In many cases, life during the Depression meant the difference between having a place to live, even if it belonged to someone else and was little more than a

Tenant farmers rest in front of their home in South Carolina. Many farmers of the Depression lived unstable lives, with poverty and homelessness a constant fear.

It All Came Tumbling Down

These women picket in front of a Civil Works Administration building, demanding that single women be given preference in employment over married women.

shack, and being cast out by the side of the road. It meant the difference between a poor diet and starvation, between flour-sack clothing and no clothing at all.

Whether in the country or city, women who worked at home caring for their families often also had to go out looking for jobs because their husbands were either laid off or had their wages and hours cut. Some husbands left their families behind when they could not find work. Other men stayed home and kept looking for jobs, but regardless of who brought in a paycheck, the cooking, making or buying clothes, and housekeeping remained the domain of mothers and daughters.

Although women could often find jobs more easily than men because "women's work" in offices and stores was slower to dry up than men's factory jobs, women's wages were half of or less than men's. Married women, in particular, faced hostility and discrimination from employers and others who believed that if women stayed home, more jobs would be available to men.

Growing Up Early

Children did not get to be children for long during the Depression. Boys often had to drop out of school to look for work. Girls often had to quit school, too, either to get a job or to stay home with younger children while their mothers worked. Young people who could not find jobs or afford college sometimes

Young children like these boys in the rural South often gave up an education in order to bring home some extra money.

took to the road. They hitched rides or walked across the country, looking for work, a place to live, and something to eat. Homeless girls sometimes had no choice but to resort to prostitution to survive.

    Family life in the thirties was much different from today. Roles were strictly divided by gender. Men worked outside the home for money, and women were responsible for the house and children. The Depression challenged these roles as people struggled to earn enough money to live. That struggle required the help of everyone — children, women, and men. While some families survived, others were torn apart by hard times — times that were harder than any they had seen before.

It All Came Tumbling Down

A Depression-era sharecropper family. With families facing grinding poverty and unemployment, the work load of women in the home did not ease up, even if they were forced to seek work outside the home.

CHAPTER THREE

Family Roles: Men and Women Face the Depression

Women and men in the 1930s shared responsibilities for raising their families, but each had a very distinct role. The woman, by and large, was responsible for the home and everything connected with it — cleaning, cooking, raising children, washing, ironing, mending clothes, and shopping for anything she could not make at home.

Men were responsible for earning the money needed to support the family. They were expected to work hard, earn as much as they could, and bring all their money home to the family. Men often worked six days a week, and work days could be ten to twelve hours long. To be called a good worker or a good provider was the highest compliment a family man could receive.

It was harder for an African-American, Asian-American, or Latino man to provide for his family. In some areas of the country, jobs were stereotyped by race or ethnicity, just as they were by gender. In the South, working by hand in the fields was considered too hard and the pay too low for anyone but African-Americans. Along the West Coast, farmers relied on immigrants from Mexico and the Philippines to provide cheap labor and even follow the crop harvest from farm to farm without a permanent home. Japanese immigrant men were hired as gardeners and workers in plant nurseries. All these jobs paid little and offered little chance for moving up economically. Outside these segregated industries, minority men had a hard time finding jobs.

The average middle-class family in 1935 lived on $1,348 a year. A woman was expected to take whatever her husband earned and make it stretch to supply all the family's needs. She might raise food in a garden, can some of it, and buy the rest. Food was cheap, but even such inexpensive items as a 10¢ quart of milk, a 5¢ loaf of bread, or butter at 23¢ a pound stretched the budgets of many families.

Farm wives were able to raise most of the food their family needed, but they had even less cash coming in than most, and it arrived more sporadically. A weekly sale of cream or eggs might be the only steady income a farm wife could count on to buy flour, sugar, coffee, and other staples.

A 1930s "housewife" would probably buy as much of the family's clothing as she could afford — certainly shoes, coats, socks and underwear, and heavy work clothes. But many women sewed children's clothing and dresses for the girls and women. Laundry was often still done by hand, as washing machines were still relatively new inventions. Almost everything was ironed back then — not only shirts and dresses but even sheets and dishtowels. Some women even ironed their husbands' underwear!

Although housework did not require as much physical strength as some men's jobs, it was considerably more tiring than today. Appliances such as washing machines, dryers, vacuum cleaners, and electric irons were just starting to become common in homes. And in rural areas, many women had no electricity to run appliances, even if they could have afforded them.

Once a man came home from his job, his day was over. Of course, it might have been a very long day doing physically exhausting work in a factory or mill. Farmers worked in the fields until dark and often even later in the barn, doing chores. But the man's work did not extend to the house. He was not usually expected to help cook supper, wash dishes, bathe children, or put them to bed. A saying popular with women was, "Man works from dawn 'til set of sun, but woman's work is never done."

Women Working Outside the Home

Of course, as with any generalization, there were many exceptions to this picture of family life. Among the poorest families, women as well as men often worked outside the home for wages. Farm women, especially in poor rural areas of the South, often did field work along with their jobs in and around the house. Men, however, seldom worked inside the house, even when their wives helped

Homeless and jobless women sign up to live in relief camps. These camps comprised one of dozens of new and innovative social programs that emerged during the Great Depression.

with farm work or held jobs. Poor women were expected to perform their traditional work, as well as earning money to help support the family.

Almost 40 percent of African-American women worked for wages, some two million in 1930, but fewer than 20 percent of white women had jobs outside the home. Sixty percent of wage-earning African-American women worked in domestic service in private homes. Another 30 percent worked in agriculture. Because these two fields were specifically excluded from laws setting minimum wages and limiting hours, and from the Social Security law that exempted small employers, African-American women benefited little by the New Deal.

They were also among the first to lose their jobs. As incomes fell and unemployment rose, many middle-class families could no longer afford to pay for housekeeping help. Those jobs that were left were suddenly more attractive to white women who would not have taken them if their husbands were still working or if higher-paying jobs were available. African-American and other minority women, already occupying the lowest-status jobs, had nowhere lower to go and faced high unemployment. By the middle of the Depression, one-fourth of all African-American working women were on relief. But many women who had no job and no one else to support them probably never made it onto the relief roles, either, because of racial discrimination in their local relief offices.

More information is available about the experience of African-American women during the Depression than about women of other minority groups. But one study of women in San Antonio during the Depression showed that Latino women were less likely to work outside the home than African-Americans, in part because of the attitudes of Latino men who did not want their wives working away from home. Because many were recent immigrants from Mexico, they also faced a language barrier that would have made working among English-speaking Americans more difficult.

When they did work outside the home, Latino women were routinely paid less than Anglo women and sometimes less than Black women working for the same employer. Mexican immigrant women often took in "home work," usually hand sewing or shelling nuts. Both types of work were difficult, demanding, and underpaid, and their wages fell even more during the Depression. Women doing home work earned from $1.10 to $3.30 per week and often averaged less than five cents per hour.

Young women out of school had a better chance of finding jobs than their brothers, because there were more jobs available in the fields stereotyped as "women's work." These jobs paid less than the scarce manufacturing, administrative, and professional jobs open to men, but many young women supported their parents, siblings, and even grandparents on the wages they earned as clerical workers or store clerks. Girls as young as sixteen dropped out of school to support their entire family.

Most young women of the 1930s would have preferred to get married and move into a home of their own, but with so few young men employed, many young people could not afford to get married. The marriage rate in 1932 was

25 percent lower than in the late 1920s. Although some young women were willing to contribute whatever they could to their family's support, others felt exploited. Families often relied on the energy of hardworking, single women to survive, but some turned their backs on those same women if they became sick or lost their jobs.

Added Worries, Added Work

The Great Depression brought additional worry and hardship to both men and women, but it affected their roles differently. The role of a woman was to run the home and make life comfortable, both physically and emotionally, for her family. The role of a man was financial support. When he lost his job, a man lost his primary family role as well. Although he still might have the final say in family decisions, he lost the opportunity to earn self-respect and respect from others for performing his role in life. A woman whose husband lost his job kept hers; she could still earn respect for performing her homemaker role, which became even more important as pressures from outside the family increased.

One of the first effects women felt was the increase in housework. When their husbands brought home less money, women were more likely to grow and can their own food, repair old clothing rather than buy new things, and sew rather than buy whatever new clothing they could afford.

In small towns, home economists employed by the county taught women how to upholster furniture and make curtains with burlap feed sacks. It often took more work to make cheaper foods appetizing, and saving on heating bills meant more quilts and sweaters had to be made to keep the family warm. Living on a low income is generally more work than life with more financial resources.

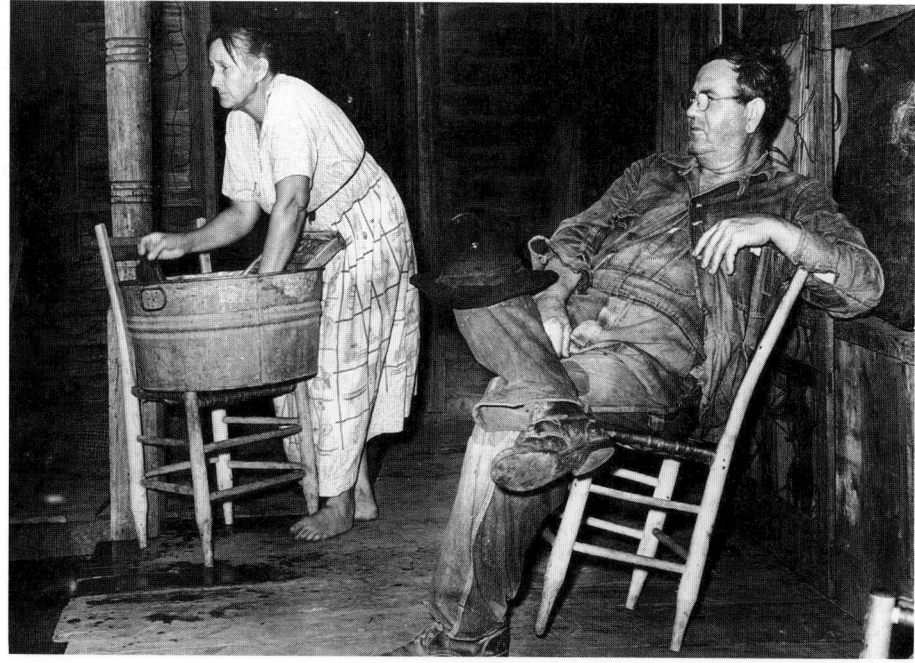

The Great Depression brought increased housework for women, whose primary role was to run the home and make life comfortable for their families, especially in the face of increased unemployment and hardship for men outside the home.

The Birth of Betty Crocker

In the 1930s, just as the Depression was cutting the food budgets of most U.S. homemakers, there was a new emphasis on the importance of the woman's role in taking care of her family. Government-supported home economists taught classes in nutrition to homemakers. A government radio program featured Aunt Sammy (Uncle Sam's "wife") giving out government-developed recipes to help women cope with limited budgets without sacrificing nutrition by making meatless meals and eggless or even flourless cakes.

Food manufacturers picked up on the trend as a way to make their products stand out. General Mills packed "kitchen-tested" recipes in their sacks of flour and claimed that 282,268 women switched to buying Gold Medal flour in just one month. The company sponsored the "Betty Crocker Hour" on the radio, with its own fictional homemaker who, like Aunt Sammy, dispensed recipes and money-saving tips.

The popularity of Betty Crocker as a symbol of the American housewife long outlasted the Depression. Today, the image of a smiling Betty Crocker wearing an apron over her dress has disappeared from the company's advertising, but you can still buy cake mixes bearing her name.

The earlier, prosperity-sparked drive toward moving more of the homemaking tasks out of the home or making them easier through labor-saving appliances was temporarily interrupted by the Depression. Canned foods had been more readily available, and convenience foods such as Jell-O, Campbell's condensed soups, and ground coffee in cans were increasingly common. But during the Depression, even urban women who were accustomed to such conveniences often went back to making everything from scratch, canning food at home, and baking their own bread.

In addition to the material needs of her family, the wife and mother of the 1930s was responsible for maintaining emotional stability. In John Steinbeck's classic novel of the Depression, *The Grapes of Wrath*, it is the women of the destitute Joad family who hold its members together and keep them from despair.

Unemployment and poverty increased tensions at home. Men who were used to being active and productive were left with nothing to do but sit around the house feeling defeated and useless. The Depression tended to increase the number of people living together to save money. Elderly parents often lived in the household, grown children sometimes had to move back in with their parents, and even adult brothers and sisters with families of their own had to share a house or apartment. Many families lived through periods without utilities when they could not pay the electric bill, and sometimes a kitchen stove was the only source of heat in the house.

Although canning had long been a traditional way to preserve fruits and vegetables, before the Depression many women had begun buying canned products from the store. When the Depression hit, however, women returned to making everything from scratch.

Family Roles

In the face of all this, women had another difficult role to play — family peacemaker. Some men became violent toward their wives and children when they could not find work. One woman said that worrying made her husband mean. He would ignore her when she called him for dinner and go on listening to the radio. But whenever they fought, she gave in to keep the peace. There were no divorces in those days, she said.

In fact, there were divorces, but there were fewer of them in the Depression for the same reason there were fewer marriages — they cost too much. Setting up separate homes was even more expensive than trying to get along in one. And it's true that divorces were far less socially acceptable in the 1930s than today, so for many people they were not a real option.

While popular images of family life in the Depression are those of families struggling together through hard times and helping each other, in fact many families were torn apart by the additional pressures. Fathers who could not support wives and children sometimes disappeared; more than one million had deserted their wives by 1932. Some committed suicide. Some lived as hoboes. For some, the only work available was in towns away from their families. Children sometimes had to go live with relatives when their parents could not support them any longer. Some separations that were intended to be temporary became permanent, and the families never recovered. Many families with strong relationships and some resources (a way to make a living, a house to live in, or relatives to help out) did seem to become even stronger in the face of adversity from the outside. But those families that were shaky to start with often did not survive.

This family was among many in a drought-stricken Arkansas community in 1931 to receive help from the American Red Cross. The boy on the right, wearing recently acquired clothing, was elated because he could return to school and receive some soup.

Losing Face: Men in the Depression

Men in the 1930s lived with social expectations as rigid as those for women. Although the role of wage earner gave them economic power and society gave them the authority to have final say on family decisions, they also lived with the expectation that they alone should be able to support a wife, children, and any other relatives that might make up the household. A man was judged by this one achievement above all others: how well he could support his family. He might be a warm, loving, responsive parent and husband, might share the burden of housework when he was at home, but those qualities did not count for much in the community if he did not hold a job. Men judged themselves by this same standard, and some became desperate enough to consider killing themselves rather than live with the shame of not providing for their families.

Minority men faced the same expectations as providers, along with the added burden of discrimination that made it even harder for them to fulfill the breadwinner role. African-American men were the last hired and first fired in most workplaces, and men from other minority groups often had no job opportunities at all aside from field work.

For them, the dream of supporting a family on their wages barely existed. Their families lived at such a low income level, and with unemployment such a regular part of their lives, that for some the Depression did not alter their lives in any significant way. They simply could not go much lower.

One Latino woman whose husband was a field worker said she had a big fight with him over continuing to move from farm to farm, following the harvest

These unemployed men idle away the hours at the slip docks in New York City. Some men became desperate and considered killing themselves rather than face the shame of unemployment.

Family Roles 41

A migrant worker in a one-room shack in New Jersey, 1938. Although joblessness and poverty affected everyone, minorities often lived at such a low income level before the Depression that the Depression did not alter their lives significantly.

season. "I tell my husband, 'This is it. No more field work. We have to educate the kids. We have to stay in one place and think about them now. . . .'" She finally settled in a town and cleaned houses to pay for her children's education.

In working- and middle-class white families, unemployment threatened men's self-esteem much more than that of women. As one woman put it, "I think hard times is harder on a man, 'cause a woman will do something. Women just seem to know where they can save or where they can help, more than a man. It's just a worry for him, and he feels so terrible when he can't take care of his family."

Because women's responsibilities were broader, they had more avenues in which to make a difference. They could use their ingenuity to make food and clothing go further at home, and if they had to, they could go out and look for a job outside the home.

Men, on the other hand, could not fulfill their duty unless they could find a job. Their role was so narrowly defined that to step out of it and find other ways to be useful to the family sometimes felt as shameful as doing nothing. One woman said that her father helped with the housework, but he was careful never to let anyone outside the family see him do it. Even though white workers would take lower-paying jobs usually reserved for minority workers, and women would take jobs usually held by men whenever they got a chance because the pay was better, men almost never took jobs identified with women.

Nursing, social work, and clerical jobs remained almost exclusively "women's work," even though men needed and wanted to work.

The first response of a man whose hours were cut or who lost his job was to search for another position. Early in the Depression, the attitude of most white people was that there must be something wrong with a man who could not find a job. But after months of futile searching, men began to lose hope and lose the will to keep on looking. They became despondent. Some ran away or killed themselves, but most simply lived through it, taking whatever short-term work they could find and going on relief if necessary, if they were fortunate enough to be accepted.

The role of asking for help in desperate situations often fell to women. Most of the letters written to the government asking for help were written by women to Eleanor Roosevelt, the First Lady. Women who begged for help to feed, clothe, and house their families, especially their children, were considered honorable because they were doing whatever was necessary to take care of their families.

For a man, on the other hand, writing to ask for help might be seen as an act of weakness. Men were supposed to be the providers of help and support, not the seekers. For this reason, the task of waiting in line for hours to apply for relief also often fell to women, though men would wait in line applying for jobs on government work projects. Applying for work was an honorable way to fill their role as breadwinner. It did not feel degrading, whereas asking for help did.

This employment agency is overflowing with men seeking work. The emotional impact of being unemployed was nearly as severe for men as the effects of losing a source of family income.

Family Roles

In front of a log cabin in Missouri, these Depression-era refugees hope to take up farming. Although farming was hard work, it ensured food on the table and a place to live.

Unemployed men in rural areas sometimes fared better, if they owned land on which they could raise food for their families. Sharecroppers, tenant farmers, and migrant workers all shared the problems of the urban unemployed, because they did not own land of their own. Farmers with mortgaged land faced the double demands of mortgage payments and property taxes, but they often needed more money for these payments than they could get from selling their crops. They did not feel the uselessness that an unemployed urban worker felt because they still had useful work to do each day. But theirs was the frustration and despair of working as hard as they could and still possibly losing everything they had.

Living Simply, Spending Little

Those who survived the Depression in the best shape were those who owned productive land and owed little or nothing on it. One woman said she and her husband lived on a farm with his parents, with no electricity or plumbing, but also without a mortgage. They raised most of what they ate, and her husband worked for thirty-five cents an hour on a neighboring farm — enough to pay their monthly grocery bill of eight dollars.

Another woman who married at fifteen lived in Missouri with her husband in a house that had no running water. But, she said, "I don't think farm people ever had the problems that city people had. We cut wood nearby, and we had a garden where we could raise something to eat. So we didn't have to be cold or hungry." Her husband also could feed his family by hunting and fishing.

The hope of independence, even at a very basic level, made the idea of moving from the city to the country very popular for poor people during the Depression. Rural areas seemed to offer more of a chance for survival than the city, but this was true only for the very hardy and those who knew how to work the land and hunt or fish. And they would never raise a family to the level of comfort enjoyed by a middle-class or even working-class urban family when jobs were available.

One lasting effect of the Depression was that the traditional roles of men and women were reinforced. By the end of the Depression, being able to support a woman at home had become a symbol of a man's success. When men went away by the thousands to fight World War II, more women worked because they had to, and the defense industry needed so many workers that they hired women for the kind of factory jobs that men traditionally held. But as soon as the men came home, they once again became their families' sole wage earner, and women returned to the traditional realm of home and family.

An illiterate squatter and sharecropper, this man doubles as a night watchman to provide the bare essentials for his family. The land around them had been so overfarmed that it could no longer provide for them.

Family Roles

A school-bound African-American boy in Savannah, Georgia. With increased responsibilities for all family members during the Depression, few children had time for their usual activities.

CHAPTER FOUR

Growing Up Fast: Children in the Great Depression

The experiences of children during the Depression varied: Some were destitute, some knew poverty but pulled through, and some barely noticed a difference in their lives. But one thing they all had in common was uncertainty and an awareness of the importance of money.

One woman said her family already lived a simple farming life, so they had most of what they needed during the Depression. "Anybody could've gotten through the Depression the way we did," she said. Working together, her father and grandfather were able to make enough money to pay the taxes and the mortgage they owed on part of their land.

"We went to town twice a year, once for school shoes and once around Christmas," she remembered. The rest of their clothing they made at home, and except for a few staples like flour and sugar that they could buy with money from selling eggs, cream, and hogs, they grew their own food.

"I remember, though," the woman recalled, "one girl who came to school wearing one black shoe and one brown one. Nobody made fun of what you wore during the Depression. We had more than some of the others, but we all thought the same — about money."

Children worried during the Depression, and they may have absorbed their parents' sense of shame or failure, but they did not feel personal guilt. They knew that what happened to their families wasn't their fault, so they escaped the feeling of failure that was one of the major psychological problems of the Depression. On the other hand, many childhoods were cut short as children were pushed into taking on adult responsibilities before they were ready. Young people with working-class parents had no time to be teenagers — in fact, that term was not even invented until later. Many girls and boys of the 1930s had to leap directly into adulthood.

Early in the Depression, boys dropped out of school to look for work. Girls dropped out to take care of younger children at home while their mothers

> **Children Asking for Help**
>
> Children shared their parents' worries during the Great Depression and wanted to help their families. But at a time when even adults could do little to improve their lives, the children had few means to change their situations. Some, in desperation, wrote to ask help from the most powerful adults they knew of — President and Mrs. Roosevelt. This letter was typical:
>
> "Dear Mr. President,
>
> "I'm a boy of 12 years. I want to tell you about my family. My father hasn't worked for 5 months. He went plenty times to relief, he filled out applications. They won't give us anything. I don't know why. Please you do something.
>
> "... My father he staying home. All the time he's crying because he can't find work. I told him why are you crying daddy, and daddy said why shouldn't I cry when there is nothing in the house. I feel sorry for him. That night I couldn't sleep. The next morning I wrote this letter to you. in my room.... Please answer right away because we need it. [We'll] starve. Thank you. God bless you."

worked, or sometimes they dropped out to get housekeeping jobs themselves. Among the poorest families, children often dropped out of school because they simply had no clothing to wear. Their dresses were too small or worn through, their pants and shirts might have had holes, and many children had no shoes. It was not a matter of style, or even of warmth, but simply a matter of decently covering their bodies. Sometimes the same clothing had to be shared by several people in the family; if a father had to go out to look for work, his son had to stay home.

Taking to the Road

While the Depression made life more difficult for children everywhere, some had been living in a depression for all of their lives. Children of migrant farm workers, for instance — most of them Mexican immigrants in Texas and the West Coast — had always worked for at least part of the year in the fields from the time they were old enough, sometimes as young as ten. They often missed at least part of the school year because they did not live in one place all year round. Mexican immigrants from Texas who traveled to Michigan to work in the sugar beet fields in the 1930s would not return until after the start of the school year, often with too little money to pay for school clothes for the children.

During the Depression, many children were uprooted from stable, if poor, farms not only by economic forces but by natural ones as well. A tremendous drought and driving winds swept across the Great

> **A New Deal: Jobs for Young People**
>
> Young people had a particularly hard time finding jobs during the Depression, especially if they had to quit school. With few skills and no experience, it was hard to compete with the many experienced people out of work. The National Youth Administration (NYA) was a New Deal program that helped by giving high school and college students part-time jobs so they could stay in school. It also provided full-time work for young people who had left school.
>
> Unlike some work programs, the NYA did a good job of helping young women as well as young men. Mary McLeod Bethune, an African-American woman, headed a Division of Negro Affairs and worked to make sure that African-Americans were hired to help run the program. As a result, African-Americans received from 10 to 20 percent of the NYA funds, a larger share than they got anywhere else during the Depression.

This Oklahoma family walks the highway in search of work and shelter. Drought and harsh winds, which swept across the Great Plains, devastated many farming families.

Plains in the 1930s during a period called the Dust Bowl. Farmers lost their crops, and the winds blew away the fertile topsoil. Poor tenant farmers could not pay their rents or feed their families.

At the same time, large landowners were beginning to buy tractors that could cheaply replace the work of tenant farmers with their teams of mules. The landowners would bulldoze the tenants' houses and plow up their yards, leaving them nowhere to live. These poor families, called "Okies" because so many came from Oklahoma, often took to the road in run-down old cars and trucks barely able to carry them and their few possessions. They headed for California, where they had heard there was plenty of work.

But when they got there, they found the work to be the same backbreaking field labor that immigrants from Mexico and the Philippines had been doing. There were far more displaced farmers and minority migrant laborers than jobs, and wages were barely enough to keep a family from starving.

Families gathered in migrant labor camps, where they lived in shacks or tents. Food was scarce, sanitation was poor, and many became sick and died. Parents, no matter how hard they worked, could never earn enough to return to a more stable life. For the children of poor field workers, school was a luxury they could only dream of returning to someday.

Growing Up Fast

This picture was taken just after these impoverished Arkansas children were given a free lunch. The classroom provided a safe and warm place for children to spend their days.

School: A Safe, Warm Place

For most U.S. families, though, school offered a better place for children to spend their days than at home. It was warm and free. With so few jobs available, high school gave young people something to do. Sometimes it even provided a hot meal, although this was not nearly as routine as it is in schools today. Very few schools in the country had school lunch programs in the 1930s, but the government did provide some 1.25 billion free lunches to low-income children in some schools. This was the beginning of the modern school lunch program.

Schools had a hard time providing enough teachers, classrooms, and books for all those students. This is because schools are supported by local government, which usually gets the money from taxes paid by local property owners. But as we saw in the cases of farmers who lost their land, many property owners, whether in the country or cities, had so little income they could not afford to pay their taxes. There was great pressure on governments to cut tax rates, which meant even less money would be available to pay for education.

Many communities could not afford to pay the teachers they already employed, let alone hire new ones. Teacher salaries were cut time and again, and even then many teachers were given vouchers instead of paychecks for the wages owed them. In Chicago, banks were supposed to buy these vouchers from the teachers, but often they did not. The teachers were literally supporting the cost of public education by continuing to work without pay. By 1932, Chicago owed its fourteen thousand teachers nearly $20 million. Finally, the situation was so bad that Chicago's teachers marched in the streets and rioted at the banks to demand they be paid.

Despite the problems communities faced during the 1930s trying to pay for public education, this was the first decade in which going to high school became the norm for American youth. At the beginning of the decade, barely half the people between ages fourteen and eighteen attended high school. After ten years of the Depression, three-fourths of American girls and boys of high school age were in school. Few of them, though, had the opportunity to go on to college.

After Childhood — What Next?

In the 1930s, the United States worried about its young people. A special issue of *Life* magazine in 1938 focused on what it called "The Youth Problem" and reported that the generation just reaching adulthood was "a sober lot." In a 1936 book called *The Lost Generation*, author Maxine Davis said, "The depression years have left us with a generation robbed of time and opportunity just as the Great War [World War I] left the world its heritage of a lost generation."

These boys are students at a Missouri school. Although a high school education became the norm for all American youth during the Depression, few children would go on to college.

The usual passageways from youth to adulthood — college, jobs, career, and marriage — seemed all but closed to the young people of the 1930s. A few slipped through — young couples married and lived with their parents, middle-class young people still occasionally managed college, and some government programs, such as the Civilian Conservation Corps (CCC) and National Youth Administration (NYA), put young people to work for a time. But for many, the dreams they had once held slipped away in the grim light of the Depression.

Betty Coed and Joe College

Not all young people lost all their dreams, however. Since the 1920s, college had been an increasingly common rite of passage into adulthood for white, middle-class young men and women. African-Americans and other minorities, too, were attending college and moving into professional careers in small but increasing numbers. Although the Depression cut their numbers, some young adults from middle-class homes still managed to scrape up the $25-per-semester tuition at state-supported land-grant universities. Few could afford the $1,000-per-year tuition required by private eastern schools, and even there, students had a harder time paying for meals and other expenses than before the Depression.

The NYA helped many young people stay in school by giving colleges grants to hire students for part-time jobs. The NYA helped more than two million high school and college students stay in school, and it was more even-handed in its distribution of funds than any other New Deal agency. Approximately half the students aided by the NYA were women, and 10 to 20 percent were African-American, their numbers rising late in the decade as more private jobs opened for white youths.

Even a college education, however, did not provide an escape from the ethnic and sexual discrimination that was woven into the fabric of American society in the 1930s. One young Japanese-American woman who came of age during the Depression recalled how she was refused a high school prize for public speaking because she was Japanese-American and the contest's sponsors were the Native Sons and Daughters of the Golden West. She got to college only to find that "Things I could major in were limited because counselors told me I wouldn't be able to find jobs in many fields."

Yet her experience was better than that of many minority young people because she was befriended by two Caucasian high school teachers who helped her get to college and supported her while she was there. She also found more acceptance in college than in high school. "There were many warm friends I made there," she concluded, "and my wonderful teachers helped to heal the wounds."

Another Asian-American woman reported that, even with a college degree in economics, she was unable to find a job outside Chinatown. And yet because she worked as a store clerk, she was envied by more traditional Chinese-American women for her freedom to work and socialize outside her home.

These members of an Indian emergency conservation program clear forest roads, fell timber, and cut lumber for roads in Oregon. American Indians were given classes in basic education and were taught skills like agriculture, forestry, and animal care. Government programs were designed to provide employment for people of many social and economic backgrounds.

An American Indian woman remembers her quest for learning in the 1930s: "The Cherokees had always gone in for education. . . . I wanted to go to medical school or law school." But she remembers being discouraged by her high school counselors, whom she says "didn't really care. Number one, I was a woman; number two, I was an Indian." Her father sold a horse so she could go to business college, a popular alternative for women in the 1930s, which readied them for clerical work rather than management positions.

Children on the Road

For other young people, there seemed to be no way out of the hardships of Depression life except to leave home. As many as 250,000 young people (mostly men but some women, too), whose average age was only eighteen, simply took to the road and became "hoboes." With no job prospects, no money for college, and perhaps no high school diploma, they sought a better life, adventure, or simply a way to remove from their parents the burden of one more mouth to feed.

They rode trains, hitchhiked, and walked from town to town, looking for work, eating in soup kitchens or hobo "jungles," and sleeping in the open, in shacks near the railroad tracks, or in missions and shelters for the homeless. Sometimes whole families rode the trains, working as migrant farm laborers or just looking for a place to settle.

Growing Up Fast

"It was a dangerous, dirty life," remembered one African-American man who rode the rails for a few months when he was seventeen. Hunger was a constant problem, and so was finding a place to sleep. Almost every locality had a law that prohibited sleeping on either public land or, without the owner's permission, private land. "You'd find a place that looked safe and curl up like an animal and try to get a few hours sleep," he said. "You were always exhausted."

These laws, called "vagrancy" laws, prohibited people from staying in town unless they had ten dollars in their pockets or could show some means of support. Those without money or a job could be arrested and sentenced to jail for anywhere from a few days to three months, depending on the town.

Despite the added hardship imposed by vagrancy laws, the African-American who rode the rails at seventeen said the freedom of being able to leave a place and move on anytime you wanted became addictive. "It got into your blood," he remembered, making it hard for him to settle down and go back to a regular job or school, despite the miseries of homelessness. He found accepting authority difficult after living on his own, even for less than a year.

Hard as it was to find food on the road, clothing was even harder to get. Local charities reserved any clothing they had for local families. Vagrants, as the travelers were called, thus were not entitled to clothing from the towns they passed through. Their only real options were to beg or steal the clothing.

At least one historian, Jean Westin, has noted that towns provided places for homeless men to sleep and eat, but few women were ever seen in the soup kitchens, and free beds were not available to them. In her book about the Depression, *Making Do,* Westin talks to a woman who recalls the girl hoboes she saw traveling near Oklahoma City. From her account, it is clear that these girls had a powerful and lasting effect on her: "Hoboes passed by all the time, and if I had anything I'd feed them out on the porch. I didn't always have extra, but when the young girls would come, I'd invite them in and try to give them something — maybe a peanut butter sandwich. They were so young —

Boys and Girls on the Road

Tom Minehan, a graduate student of the 1930s, dressed as a hobo and lived among them. His reports on their conditions were published as a book titled *Boy and Girl Tramps of America.* Often, Minehan said, it was too cold to sleep at night, so children slept during the warmer daytime hours. As a result, they awoke too late to get a meal at the bread lines, and so these boys and girls might go for days at a time without a meal. Here's how Minehan described their struggle to find food: "The youth can beg on the streets, walking miles perhaps before he gets a nickel. A boy can steal, but the chances are that he will be caught. A girl can offer her body, but as likely as not she will find nobody in the market with desire and a dime. The usual course is to remain hungry until breakfast at a mission for a boy, or until breakfast can be begged by a girl. If the boy is very hungry, he may glom a grub from garbage cans."

Although thousands of migratory families fled the "Dust Bowl" of the Great Plains for California, few are as lucky as this child, who found work picking cotton in the San Joaquin Valley.

maybe twenty — maybe younger. I'd want to ask them where they were from and where they were going, but I didn't."

Most of the young women, like others on the road, probably could not have told her where they were going. Like most people during the Depression, they were not sure where they were going or how they would get there. They only hoped to survive the journey.

This photo captures a classic impression of the Great Depression: an apple seller on a New York street corner. During the Depression, many people sold apples to avoid having to beg for small change.

CHAPTER FIVE

Working in the Great Depression

The history of the Great Depression is a story about work: the kinds of work people did, how they got paid for their labor, and what happened to them when their work was taken away from them.

Work plays different roles in our lives. Sometimes work is something we would like to avoid. But often work is rewarding. It can give lives shape and purpose and be a means of self-expression. Children and adults enjoy the feeling of accomplishment and of being productive that comes from performing a job well. Finally, most people have to work to earn money to buy what they need and want. Having shelter, food, and clothing depends on having the opportunity and ability to work.

Working out of necessity is what most people were worried about during the Great Depression. Even those who had jobs were worried about losing them. And while most American adults were working at any given time, many lost some of the income from their jobs through cuts in pay and work hours.

Working in Rural America

In the 1930s, many more Americans lived and worked on farms than today. One-fourth of all jobs were in farming in 1929. During World War I, the government encouraged farmers to raise more crops to export to Europe, where the war was being fought. Banks lent farmers money to buy more land, and some went deeply into debt.

Then, in the 1920s, when Europe recovered from World War I and no longer needed to import much food, U.S. farm prices fell. At the same time, farmers were beginning to buy tractors and modern machinery. Not only could they cultivate more land, but the 25 million acres of farm land needed for feeding horses and mules could now be planted with food crops. This caused a crop and food surplus, which pushed prices down even further.

Farmers were the first to feel the effects of the Great Depression. Farm income started to fall in the late 1920s, and by 1932 it was less than one-third its 1929 level, when it was already low. Banks began foreclosing on (taking back) farms when farmers could not repay the loans they had used to buy their

How Some Farm Families Survived

Not every farmer lost his or her farm in the Depression. Those who owned their own land, livestock, and equipment (the *capital* necessary to produce goods) often survived even when farm prices were so low. One strategy for making money was to use the cheaper farm products to feed the livestock or the family and sell only those items that brought the most money.

"My mother always said we made money during the Depression," one midwestern woman recalled. "We separated the [cream from the] milk and sold the cream. Some of the milk we fed to the hogs, so we always had good fat hogs that way. We let some of the milk sour, and fed it to the chickens. [Milk is rich in the calcium chickens need to produce strong egg shells.] The hatchery always wanted our eggs, because they were so good."

Another woman who lived with her in-laws in New England during the Depression remembered keeping the insect-damaged vegetables to eat at home and selling all the perfect produce for cash.

land and equipment. Even farmers who owned their farms sometimes lost their land when they could pay their property taxes.

When Franklin Roosevelt took office in 1933, he believed that raising farm prices would be enough to end the Depression. He and others believed that part of the problem was that farmers were producing too much food. They tried to lower farm production by paying farmers to produce less and by destroying crops they had already planted. So although millions of people were hungry, the government slaughtered hogs and sheep and plowed under millions of acres of food crops. This lowered the supply of food, but it did nothing for the people who could not afford to buy food even when it was so cheap. It also did not raise farm prices, because the program was voluntary, and some farmers took their poorest land out of production but planted more on their better land. At the same time, the program had a devastating effect on many tenant farmers.

A tenant farmer family in a Maryville, California, migrant camp during the peach season.

58 *A Multicultural Portrait of the Great Depression*

African-American tenant farmers plant peanuts on a farm in Georgia. Most African-Americans, too poor to own their own land, became sharecroppers for wealthy land owners.

No Land of Their Own: Tenant Farmers

Among our most enduring images of poverty in the United States are the pictures and stories of tenant farmers during the Great Depression. Some were tied to the land and trapped in hopeless poverty; others were forced to leave with nowhere to go. Their lives were documented by some of the finest artists of the time: photographers Dorothea Lange and Walker Evans, writer James Agee, and novelist John Steinbeck, among others.

After the Civil War, southern plantation owners had devised a new way to keep their positions of power and maintain their wealth. Most African-Americans and many whites were too poor to own their own land and had no money to rent it. Plantation owners, called planters, needed workers to farm their land, so they would let poor farmers live on and farm a small section of the plantation. At the end of the harvest, the tenant farmer would pay rent in cash or with a large portion of the crop. This system was called sharecropping.

Because sharecroppers did not have money to live on until the crops were sold, the landowners would let them buy food and other necessities on credit at the local country store — which was also often owned by the landowner. The tenants were charged high rates of interest on any money they owed the store, and some landowners would not let their tenants plant gardens or raise animals, so they would be forced to buy everything they needed from the store. Prices for seed, fertilizer, food, and clothing were higher at these country stores than at others in town.

Working in the Great Depression

A New Deal: Working in the Woods

Early in Roosevelt's first one hundred days in office, he created one of the most successful and best-remembered New Deal programs, the Civilian Conservation Corps (CCC). The program took thousands of young men who otherwise would have been on relief, housed them in military-style camps in the woods, fed them, provided some education and vocational training, and gave them jobs in reforestation and on fire and flood-control projects. This work had long-term benefits for many people. And though the pay was low, about twenty-five dollars a month, and the life regimented, for most young men, life in the camps was better than what they had left behind at home.

But the program could have helped more people than it did. CCC offered nothing for the young women across the country who were working to support their parents, brothers, and sisters. And it also missed an opportunity to help young minority men, who had the poorest job prospects and greatest need for food, clothing, and housing.

Like the military of the time, the CCC remained strictly segregated, and only 3 percent of its first quarter-million enrollees were African-American. Although eventually the number of minorities enrolled in CCC equalled their percentage of the population, the CCC's enrollment policies never truly considered the greater needs of minorities. One state CCC director from the South explained his reason for including so few Blacks: "There are few Negro families who need an income as great as twenty-five dollars a month." Besides, he said, Black field hands were depended on for planting and chopping cotton. Because those jobs paid too little for whites to take them, the South's farming economy depended on cheap Black labor.

By harvest time, sharecroppers or tenant farmers often owed the landlord more than their crops earned. At best, they might earn a profit too small to carry their families through the next year, and so they remained in debt to the landlord. Planters often told sharecroppers they had to stay on the farm until they paid what they owed, even though this was illegal. But the planters, the local sheriffs, and the judges of the South were interested in helping each other stay in power, not in helping poor people get justice or improve their lives. And so tenant farmers and sharecroppers had no power to fight the system.

In the 1930s, one-fourth of the population of the South still lived and worked as sharecroppers or tenant farmers. The government's crop-reduction program was a disaster for them. It forced many of them to leave the homes they did not own, with no money, no job, and nowhere to go.

When the government paid landowners not to plant crops, the owners no longer needed tenant farmers and sharecroppers. The law said the landowners were supposed to pass along to their tenants a small percentage of their government payment, but many landowners kept the full payment for themselves. To correct this, the program was later changed to send the tenants their shares directly. But even this did not help tenants, because it gave landlords another reason to evict them from their homes. Without tenant farmers or sharecroppers, landowners could receive the full payment themselves.

Although the program did raise farm prices by 50 percent during FDR's first term, it was not enough to even solve the problems of farmers, much less end the Depression.

The Dust Bowl

The government's program to cut crop production was not the only reason food supplies fell and prices rose. A severe drought started in 1934, and by the next year, the United States had to import wheat. Along with the lack of rain, terrible winds roared across Texas, Oklahoma, and Kansas. Where prairie grasses had once held the soil against the winds of the Great Plains, years of repeated plowing and planting in the late nineteenth and early twentieth centuries

An abandoned farm house in Texas during the time of the "Dust Bowl," when wind and years of plowing and planting seriously weakened the land.

Working in the Great Depression

On their trek through Texas in 1936, these Dust Bowl refugee family members stop to repair the truck that transports them and their belongings.

loosened the dirt and left it vulnerable to the dry winds. Storms whipped the topsoil into clouds that blackened the sky and ruined productive farms.

This drought was called the Dust Bowl, and it caused not only higher farm prices but also a major disruption of life in the Great Plains and Midwest. Small farmers with mortgages and taxes could not pay their bills because their crops dried up in the fields. Tenant farmers who in good years raised just enough to feed their families and pay the rent could not keep up with the rent during the drought.

At the same time, the availability of new farming equipment put many tenant farmers out of business. Landowners discovered that with tractors and modern farm implements, they could hire one person to farm hundreds of acres, or they could do the work themselves. They did not need tenant farmers working small plots of land with their teams of mules. Many landowners even tore down the tenants' houses and barns and planted that land, too. Thousands of poor farmers and their families lost their homes in this way, and many headed for California in hopes of finding work. As we saw, most of them found nothing but poverty worse than what they had left behind.

The Plight of Immigrant Farm Workers

Before the Dust Bowl, the backbreaking labor of hand planting and picking food crops was done by immigrants. Many of these were from Mexico; some had lived in this country for years and had children born here who were U.S. citizens. Others were from Asian countries, especially the Philippines.

Filipino Workers. From 1898 to the start of World War II, the Philippines was a U.S. territory, and its people were considered U.S. nationals, though not full citizens. In the 1920s, the Filipinos, or Pinoys, as they called themselves, were encouraged to come work on Hawaiian plantations and the huge farms of the West Coast.

Almost all the Filipino immigrants were men who lived together in migrant labor camps where they were paid very little and given hard "stoop" work by white and Japanese farmers. They were considered hardly human; it was thought they did not suffer from long hours bending low in the fields because they were short and, unlike other men, did not feel the itchiness of the peat dust on their sweaty skin. They lived in cold and drafty bunkhouses without adequate water for washing.

A great backlash developed against immigrant workers during the Great Depression, a time when European-American workers were available to fill almost any job. Racism was a powerful force driving discrimination against the Filipinos, whose skin was brown. They were often refused service in restaurants and stores and called "monkey" or "little brown brother." Lonely for female companionship and lacking Filipino women to marry, Pinoys had begun to date and marry white women. Laws were passed that prevented Filipino men from becoming U.S. citizens, prohibited them from marrying European-American women, and excluded them from receiving relief under New Deal programs.

Another reason Filipino farm workers became unpopular with their bosses was that they were prepared to fight for better working conditions more than many other immigrants. They formed the Filipino Labor Union (FLU) and in 1933 struck for higher wages, but farmers brought in Mexican, East (Asian) Indian, and Japanese workers to break the strike. In 1934, the FLU struck lettuce growers for higher pay and held out in the face of violence and police brutality to achieve its goals. Then, in 1936, the FLU led another strike and formed a combined union with Mexican workers that became part of the powerful American Federation of Labor (AFL).

By 1935, American growers were ready to be rid of the Filipinos they had once sought as cheap labor. Congress passed the Repatriation Act, offering to send Filipinos who were receiving charitable support back to the Philippines at government expense if they gave up the right to ever come back. Few chose to go; returning at government expense without their own money was considered an admission of failure by most Filipinos.

Deportation of Mexican Workers and Families. Mexican farm laborers performed much of the same underpaid field work as Filipinos and faced similar discrimination. Yet their lives differed in one important way: Many Mexican women as well as men migrated to the United States, worked in the fields, and raised families.

During the Depression, when tenant farmers and other destitute people flooded California looking for any kind of work, many farmers stopped hiring

> **Finding Words for the Pain**
>
> One Filipino immigrant who suffered in the fields of California was brutally beaten for helping to organize farm workers and later became a writer as a means of fighting injustice. His name was Carlos Bulosan. Having experienced both the violence and cruelty of racism in the United States and the human warmth and generosity he had expected to find in this country, Bulosan struggled to understand how one society could encompass both. As he traveled the country in the 1930s and met others suffering poverty and discrimination, he came to a conclusion — recorded in an account of his travels and observations called *America Is in the Heart* — that the United States is not a land of one race or one class of people: "We are all Americans that have toiled and suffered and known oppression and defeat, from the first Indian that offered peace in Manhattan to the last Filipino pea pickers.... America is also the nameless foreigner, the homeless refugee, the hungry boy begging for a job and the black body dangling on a tree."

Mexican immigrants and Mexican-Americans. These migrant workers and their families turned to the cities, and when they could not find work there, they joined other poor families on the welfare roles.

During the Depression, U.S. cities were close to bankruptcy and looking for any way possible to save money. Officials in many cities decided it would be cheaper to send Mexicans back to Mexico than to pay their welfare expenses. They did not pay attention to whether a person was a Mexican immigrant or a Mexican-American who was born in the United States or had become a naturalized citizen. Many people who had a legal right to stay in this country were "repatriated" (sent back to their country of origin), even though they were not citizens of Mexico.

People of Mexican descent were uprooted from their lives in this country simply for being poor. Los Angeles sent at least fifteen thousand welfare recipients to Mexico on fifteen special trains between 1931 and 1934. Among those deported were children who had grown up in the United States and were leaving behind their friends and communities. One girl remembered thinking longingly of her high school in Los Angeles as the train she rode pulled into Mexico City.

The city of Detroit established in its Public Welfare Department in 1932 a Mexican Bureau, which arranged for trains to carry Mexicans to the U.S.-Mexico border for fifteen dollars per person, including food. Mexicans and Mexican-Americans who applied for welfare payments were pressured into saying they wanted to go to Mexico, and their protests to the contrary were ignored. Other U.S. cities deported Mexicans as well, and as word spread through the Mexican-American community, people became afraid even to apply for welfare.

The practice became widespread, though no official records were kept of the total number deported. Neither is it known how many Mexican immigrants actually did return voluntarily to their homeland when jobs in the United

States became scarce. We do know that the number of people living in this country who were born in Mexico dropped from 639,000 in 1930 to 377,000 ten years later.

The Indian New Deal

Native Americans were so desperately poor even before the Depression that in 1928, half their population lived on an annual income of one hundred to two hundred dollars per person. Other Americans that year earned an average of nearly $1,350. By 1933, American Indians' income had fallen to eighty-one dollars per person. While Congress was spending money to help other Americans in need, it also agreed to help Native Americans.

Of all the programs labeled as part of the New Deal, the most effective was probably the "Indian New Deal." Though named after other programs of the Roosevelt administration, the Indian New Deal actually had little in common with other relief programs. Although it included emergency relief, the Indian New Deal also reversed government policies that had, since colonial times, been trying to destroy Native American culture.

Emergency programs distributed food and created government jobs. An Indian Civilian Conservation Corps (a separate program modeled after the CCC but run by a different agency) hired Native people to plant trees on reservation lands where forests had been cut, stop soil erosion by building terraces and dams, guard forests against fire, build roads, reseed ranges, and generally improve their own lands. Indian CCC camps included whole families. Government teachers gave classes for both adults and children in basic education and taught skills like agriculture, forestry, and animal care.

Other parts of the Indian New Deal showed a big shift in government attitudes toward Native Americans. Since colonial days, the United States had been trying to persuade or force American Indians to give up their land and their culture and become "Americanized." The Indian New Deal changed this policy. It gave land back to tribal groups and provided money to buy back other lost tribal lands. It ended the practice of sending Indian children to government boarding schools, where they would be punished for speaking their own languages, and made Indian education bilingual. It helped tribes start businesses so

An American Indian woman and her child at a forest camp in the Warm Springs Reservation in Oregon, where Native people were hired to plant trees, stop soil erosion, and generally improve their own land.

Working in the Great Depression

American Indian children at the Indian Emergency Conservation Camp in Oregon.

their members could support themselves and protected their right to practice their own cultural traditions and religions.

One of the most important changes the Indian New Deal made was to let tribes set up their own governments and choose leaders to run them. This meant that for the first time, the United States government recognized Native Americans' right to self-rule. The law making this change even specified that tribes could refuse to set up governments if they so chose.

The Indian New Deal did not undo all the damage done by hundreds of years of violence, oppression, and neglect to Native people. But it did mark a drastic turnaround for U.S. policy toward American Indians, recognizing their rights and moving to redress some wrongs.

Work in Cities and Towns

Many people were forced to leave poor rural areas during the Great Depression and seek work in cities and towns. It was a decade when a wave of African-Americans moved from southern plantations to northern cities, hoping to find work that paid better and gave them a fair chance in life. Poor white farmers left the land, too, when prices were so low they could not support their families anymore. But while more jobs were available in the cities than on farms, there were not enough jobs for everyone.

At times during the Depression, 25 percent of the workforce was unemployed. One in every four workers who wanted a job could not find one — as many as fifteen million people in 1933, when the Depression was at its worst.

A New Deal: Better Than No Work at All

Both the FDR administration and most relief recipients preferred work relief — government jobs created to employ the jobless — to straight relief payments. Jobs preserved the self-respect of the recipient and eliminated the fear that people would prefer relief payments to working for a living. But relief job wages were kept very low (so the government would not compete with private employers), and workers were often limited in the number of hours they could work. As a result, relief jobs barely provided enough income to live on, but they were better than nothing at all, and many people competed for them.

The various work programs are some of the best known of the New Deal, and they are considered to be some of the most successful. The Civil Works Administration (CWA) was a short-lived program designed to provide as many jobs as possible to low-skilled workers during the winter of 1933-34, when unemployment was severe and FDR had just taken office. CWA was the most successful employment program, but it was abandoned after one winter because businesspeople and southern farmers complained that CWA competed for cheap labor, and government officials worried about its cost. The Public Works Administration (PWA), created in 1933, built bridges, dams, school buildings, hospitals, city buildings, and other public facilities.

Perhaps the biggest and most famous work relief program was the Works Progress Administration (WPA) started in 1935, which helped many Americans get through the later years of the Depression. Although it never provided jobs for more than one-third of those unemployed, it still helped more people survive the Depression than any other government program. It is also the program that employed the writers, musicians, artists, and theater professionals discussed in Chapter One.

There were some advantages to the low prices of the Depression years. Although people did not make much money, it also took very little to buy what they needed. With a few dollars saved or borrowed from relatives, a person could start a small business.

One man started a produce business in a small town, buying and selling chickens, eggs, and butter, with $79.45 of his own, plus $20.00 borrowed from a brother. He recorded his expenses on the first day of business, January 1, 1933: truck, $40.00; chicken coops, $6.50; scales, $5.00; egg cases, $2.50; Hoover (vacuum cleaner), $5.00; windows, $10.00; poultry purchase, $3.76; butter purchase (10 pounds @ 23¢/lb.), $2.30; egg purchase (3 dozen @ 20¢/doz.), 60¢.

Small businesses like this one often made just enough money to support a family, sometimes with added income from other jobs. This man stayed in business this way until the mid-1940s, when he took another big step and opened a general store at a country crossroads.

Working in the Great Depression

Getting Ahead During the Depression

Although African-Americans faced job discrimination even in northern cities, the Depression offered some a chance to buy property they could not have afforded during prosperous times.

One woman recalled how, when she moved to Chicago in the 1930s, only unskilled jobs were available to her, though she was trained as a teacher. But as she and her husband were both working, they found a way to get ahead: "We rented in this building until 1935 . . . then we started buying it and eventually another one as well. One building helped pay for the other that way. Many of our friends were doing the same thing. We knew that a depression was on and it was the time to try to get ahead if you could. We used to talk about how to do it. Prices were down and property was cheap. It was the best time to buy some security for the future."

Discrimination Against African-Americans and Women

For African-Americans, unemployment was far higher than the national average of 25 percent. In 1932, Black unemployment stood at 50 percent. Racial discrimination accounted for the difference. African-Americans were the last hired and first fired in many industries, and they began to be laid off from their jobs as early as 1929. As jobs became scarce for white people, they, too, wanted any work at all — even jobs traditionally considered too hard, dirty, or poorly paid for white people. African-Americans were often fired so their jobs could be given to out-of-work white people.

In the South, violence against African-Americans increased. Racist European-Americans blamed African-Americans for the lack of jobs, and some resented them holding any jobs at all. As a result, the number of lynchings grew from eight in 1932 to twenty-eight the following year and remained high through the middle of the decade. One white group in Atlanta promoted the slogan, "No Jobs for Niggers Until Every White Man Has a Job," and one man from Georgia wrote to the president complaining about "Negroes being worked ever where instead of white men it don't look like that is rite. . . ."

Women faced discrimination in hiring, too. Jobs used to be segregated by sex, and newspaper ads listed jobs under either "Help Wanted, Male" or "Help Wanted, Female." There were two to three times more ads for men than women in a typical Sunday newspaper in the 1930s. Jobs advertised included factory positions, engineering, sales — a wide variety. For women, the scope was narrower. "Girl, over 17, for general housekeeping. Room and board, small wages. Nice home," a typical ad might read. Housekeeping was listed the most often, followed by sales of various products, such as "run-proof silk hosiery" or cosmetics. Women sold these products door-to-door or through home demonstrations, earning commissions on sales rather than a guaranteed salary or wage.

A group of unemployed New Yorkers pass the time.

Frances Perkins, secretary of labor, surveys the Golden Gate Bridge project in San Francisco, California, in 1935. Government-created projects like this one provided jobs to many people who would otherwise have been unemployed during the Great Depression.

Another difference between ads for women and for men was the requirements listed for women. The first requirement for women, as for men, was experience, especially when commercial employers, such as factories, bakeries, or hotels, advertised for female help. But unlike in ads for men, these and other employers also often asked for women of a certain age: "girl over 20," "woman 25-35," or "middle-aged woman," depending on the type of job.

Women were also sometimes judged by employers on personal rather than professional qualities, such as appearance or personality. One employer looking for a woman to do bookkeeping advertised for an "attractive girl." Others specified "attractive personality." That housekeepers and companions were expected to be "neat and clean" was perhaps a more reasonable requirement.

Another qualification often demanded of women in the 1930s, though often not stated in employment ads, was that they be single. Job applicants were routinely asked their marital status, and married women would often be refused a job on that basis.

As we saw when we looked at family life, there was widespread feeling against married women working if their husbands were working or capable of working, whether or not they had a job or their wages would support a family. This was true regardless of whether the woman had a professional career. One letter writer of 1936 complained to President Roosevelt, "I know that something can be done about the married women who are working in factories, department stores and offices. They have no right taking the jobs and

Working in the Great Depression   69

positions of single girls, single men and married men. . . . If the married woman is put out of business, it will make room for many unemployed men and women. . . ."

Even government policies supported this view. Federal offices that had to cut staff were required to first fire those whose spouses also worked for the government. Married women could not get jobs on federal work relief projects if their husbands were capable of working, and several states passed legislation that also created barriers to working for married women. Seventy-seven percent of the school districts in the country would not hire married women teachers, and half the districts fired women when they got married. Many private companies and 43 percent of public utilities fired all their married women employees and refused to hire new ones.

Even some women themselves believed that married women shouldn't be competing with single women and men for jobs. One Kansas teacher reported that she quit her job during the Depression because her husband was working and they had no children; she knew some man with a family would need her job. A single woman wrote to Frances Perkins, secretary of labor, in 1937: "I am a girl 23 years old have to make a living and can't get a job. . . . I think our government should pass a law so that married women can not be employed in factories or stores, that would give the single girl a chance to get a job. I think the single girl is entitled to make [a] living more so than the married woman who has a husband to support her and mostly they work so they can buy a lot [of] luxuries."

This was a common myth. But most married women worked to feed their children and themselves, often along with an unemployed or sick husband and parents.

Some people simply opposed any women working. Writer Norman Cousins highlighted the simplistic nature of this argument in 1939: "There are approx-

Better Than Raising Babies

Harsh as factory conditions were in the 1930s, some women preferred them to the demands of raising children and keeping house. One woman, who at age fourteen had gone to work in a cotton mill, told a government worker during the Depression that she liked factory work much better than life at home as oldest daughter of a poor farmer:

"I loved the mill from the start. It was such a change from keepin' house, and tendin' to babies. I just had to keep my mind on one thing then: tyin' knots. I could do it without thinkin' and that was what I needed. I'd been lookin' after babies since I was three years old."

Though she never wanted children, she married at seventeen and before long had two babies. When she felt they were old enough, she went back to the mill and got a job. Though she was happy, her husband was not, he had promised himself when they married that whe would never have to work in the mill again.

"It was the hardest thing in the world," she said, "to make him see that I'd a heap rather work in the mill than to do what I was doing."

imately 10,000,000 people out of work in the United States today; there are also 10,000,000 or more women, married and single, who are jobholders. Simply fire the women, who shouldn't be working anyway, and hire the men. Presto! No unemployment. No relief rolls. No depression."

Of course, people who held that view did not explain how they expected all those women to eat and pay their rent. Nor did they account for the fact that many of the people out of work were also women who had been employed and needed to be again. They held to a simplistic belief that all women needed or wanted to survive were working husbands, and that these men were available to any women who wanted them.

Boycotts and Rioting in Harlem

New York City in the 1930s was rigidly divided by race, yet it represented to many African-Americans a place of comparative freedom and opportunity. Many rural and southern Black people moved to New York during the 1920s and 1930s, where they settled in the African-American community, Harlem. Though strictly segregated by landlords who would not rent to Black people in any other part of the city, African-Americans created a vibrant social and cultural life that attracted people from other areas of the city to Harlem's theaters and nightclubs. This period, which reached its height during the 1920s, was called the Harlem Renaissance.

Within Harlem, African-American doctors, dentists, attorneys, teachers, and other professionals could practice and serve their community. But for less-educated Black workers, few semi-skilled or skilled jobs existed. Most of the real estate and businesses in Harlem were owned by white people, who would only hire African-Americans to do cleaning, serve as door attendants, and perform

This New York City police officer stops a man in Harlem during racial disturbances in the 1930s.

Working in the Great Depression 71

other service jobs. White-collar managerial jobs, and even sales clerk positions, were reserved for white people. In 1934, there were so few African-American sales clerks in Harlem stores that the local newspaper heralded the news that there was "another Negro Clerk in 125th Street."

In June 1934, Harlem residents began a boycott of a major department store that did not employ Black salespeople. They refused to buy goods from a store where they could not work, and after six weeks, the store agreed to hire African-American women as clerks. But even this hiring proved discriminatory, as the store chose the lightest-skinned people it could find, and disagreements arose between light- and dark-skinned people in the community.

Nevertheless, the successful boycott led to others, and more African-Americans found jobs in the stores where they shopped. Then, in 1935, rumors spread that an African-American boy had been killed for shoplifting. Harlem erupted in a riot against white-owned stores, and when it was over, many more stores agreed to hire African-Americans.

A man is taken away by police following riots that raged in Harlem after a rumor spread that an African-American boy was killed for shoplifting. After the riots, some white-owned stores agreed to hire African-Americans.

Working in the Factories

Like the citizens of Harlem, many American factory workers in the 1930s were treated unfairly. Urban workers had to depend on business owners to hire them, and at a time when there were more workers than jobs, the owners had the advantage. They could cut wages, demand long work days and weeks, refuse to provide safe or healthy working conditions, and fire people for any reason they chose, whether because of illness or marriage, or because the owner simply wished to hire someone else instead.

Working conditions in factories were so bad that many workers compared their jobs to slavery. They were afraid to protest because there were plenty of unemployed people waiting to take their jobs if they were fired. Yet many wrote to the federal Department of Labor asking for improved working conditions. One letter writer said her husband "worked 30 hours without stopping only to 'gulp' a few bites and watched the [factory machine] motor while he did that, then he came home at 2 o'clock, bathed & went to bed and at 7 that evening they wanted him to go back and work again and they never paid him an extra dime. From Monday to Friday one man only had 4 hrs. off duty so he said and never got any extra pay."

"They are so mean to their help," this woman concluded, "those who don't have to have work won't stay, but if one has a family they must do something but this is slavery."

The answer she received to her letter was that the government could not regulate work hours and wages unless new legislation was passed. An earlier attempt had been declared invalid by the Supreme Court. Eventually, Congress did pass wage and hour legislation, but until then, the only help for workers would come from the workers themselves.

Workers Rebel

As the Filipino and Mexican farm workers found out, the only way to demand better working conditions was to unite. If everyone refused to work unless conditions changed, the employer would be forced to negotiate with the workers or shut down the business. The organizations that formed to unite workers were called labor unions.

Until the 1930s, few U.S. workers were protected by labor unions. Those that existed mostly represented skilled workers; together these unions formed the powerful American Federation of Labor (AFL). But the AFL was not interested in organizing the thousands of unskilled laborers who worked in the newer factories. AFL leaders and their members considered themselves better than the average unskilled worker; they excluded African-Americans, women, and ethnic minorities from membership.

By 1935, factory workers were so angry at the conditions under which they worked that they began demanding that the unions represent them, too, and Congress finally passed a law protecting the rights of workers to form and join unions without being fired by their employers.

Some smaller union organizations, including communist labor organizations formed by people who promoted workers' rights and social equality regardless of race or gender, were making progress in organizing unskilled workers. But many Americans were afraid that communist unions would lead to the formation of a communist government like the one in the Soviet Union. And many white American men were strongly opposed to equal rights for minorities and women.

Employers used this fear to discredit labor organizers by calling them "communist agitators," regardless of their political beliefs. Workers in the Great Depression were often desperate enough to support radical changes in society and certainly to demand more control over their work lives. But the fear of losing their democratic freedoms, or of being thought of as disloyal to the United States, kept most workers from joining unions led by communists and others with "radical" or "leftist" political beliefs.

The most significant step forward for unskilled factory workers came when some leaders within the AFL began organizing workers by industry instead of by job skill. Soon these leaders and unskilled union members were expelled from the AFL and founded their own Congress of Industrial Organizations (CIO), an umbrella organization of cooperating unions similar to the AFL.

The first big CIO strike was against three giant rubber manufacturers in Akron, Ohio. One company told workers they would have to work eight hours instead of six every day for the same pay. In early 1936, the workers at all three companies struck. The strikers used a new tactic called the sit-down strike. They essentially took over the factories, sitting down at their machines so that replacement workers, called "scabs," could not be brought in.

The strikers were eventually successful, and the CIO would go on to make many more gains for workers in the auto industry and elsewhere. Formation of the CIO, which for the most part did not discriminate against women or minorities, may have had a more lasting, beneficial effect for most U.S. workers than all the government's New Deal programs.

It would be another two years before Congress passed the Fair Labor Standards Act, the first law to protect workers from inhumane and unfair treatment. It set minimum wages and maximum work weeks and outlawed child labor in most industries, a promising beginning but not enough to make the lives of workers much easier. The law also failed to protect some of the most vulnerable workers — poor people employed on farms and in domestic service.

Yet the Fair Labor Standards Act did establish, for the first time, that workers had rights to decent working conditions and fair payment for their work and that they expected their government to uphold those rights. For all working Americans, this was a big step forward.

The End of the Depression

The government's New Deal, for all its promises and goals and new ideas, did not end the Great Depression. It took World War II and the huge increase in defense spending that put every able-bodied person to work to really get the economy moving again. Instead of pouring money into making bridges, roads, hospitals, museums, parks, apartments, music, theater, books, and art, the government spent it on military payrolls and on building ships, planes, and weapons. The demand for products and services needed to fight World War II created thousands of new jobs. After the Japanese bombed the U.S. military base at Pearl Harbor, Hawaii, on December 7, 1941, and the United States entered the war, the country rapidly pulled out of the Depression.

Yet the Depression and the New Deal had perhaps the most far-reaching effect on U.S. society of any event in the twentieth century. Government began taking a more active role in the lives of its citizens, creating a welfare system to keep people from going hungry. It also created Social Security to help the elderly, children, the unemployed, and people who were sick or disabled. For the first time, government supported farmers by setting minimum prices for their crops. Government guaranteed the right of workers to form labor unions and required business to bargain fairly with striking workers. And Congress passed new laws to protect employees from unfair practices, outlaw child labor, set minimum wages, and make a standard work week no more than forty hours long.

Most of the political partnerships and practices formed in the Great Depression lasted fifty years and more before they began to be questioned. Americans divided themselves into the haves and the have-nots, and the working class supported the party of the New Deal, the Democratic Party. African-Americans deserted the Republican Party — the party of Abraham Lincoln — during the Depression, and it was the promises of another great president, Franklin D. Roosevelt, a Democrat, that wooed them away. FDR was such an accomplished politician that Democrats and Republicans alike have studied his methods ever since. He communicated directly to the American people in a way that no previous president had and that politicians today still emulate.

A half-century later, the effects of the Great Depression are fading. Its solutions to social problems are beginning to be questioned, and few people remember the lessons their parents and grandparents learned about the importance of savings and the dangers of living on credit. Yet looking back at the Depression helps us understand much of the rest of the century, the ideas that governed our history, shaped our culture, and became fixed in our national identity.

Wearing a sign board advertising meals for one cent, this man offers an example of how inexpensive a "deluxe" meal was during the 1930s. He also presents a classic Depression image of people eager to find a job.

Working in the Great Depression

CHRONOLOGY

1918 World War I ends; soldiers come home to raise families; European countries import food from U.S. farmers, who borrow money to buy more land and equipment

1920s Demand for houses, cars, and appliances soars; jobs are plentiful, and wages are good

1927 Farm prices start to fall; Europe can raise its own food again

1929 In September, stock market prices start to decline; on October 24, the New York Stock Exchange crashes; the Great Depression begins; among the first to lose their jobs are African-Americans

1930 Miniature golf is invented and sweeps the country as a way for worried, but not yet unemployed, Americans seek to escape the growing bad news

1931 As jobs become scarcer for white Americans, Los Angeles begins sending welfare recipients of Mexican descent to Mexico; over fifteen thousand Mexican-Americans are "repatriated" to Mexico, regardless of their citizenship, from Los Angeles alone by 1934

1932 Major effects of the Great Depression become apparent across the nation: family life suffers as millions lose their jobs; over one million fathers have deserted their families because they couldn't support them; marriage rate has dropped by one-fourth since the Depression began, because many young people cannot afford to set up housekeeping; Chicago owes its teachers twenty million dollars in back pay; farmers earn less than one-third what they did in 1929; African-American unemployment reaches 50 percent; in November, Americans who blame Republican president Herbert Hoover for not doing enough to end their suffering elect Franklin D. Roosevelt, a Democrat, to the presidency; March 4: Roosevelt takes office; he declares a "bank holiday" so people cannot withdraw all their money and force the banks out of business; to calm the public's fear, Roosevelt gives his first "fireside chat," broadcast on national radio. The next day, the banks reopen and the immediate bank crisis is over

1933 The worst and possibly the most eventful year of the Depression: 15 million people — one-fourth of the workforce — are out of work; more than 16 million people — half the U.S. population — own radios; lynchings of African-Americans in the South grow as white people look for someone to blame; twenty-eight lynchings are reported in 1933, twenty more than in 1932; African-American actor Paul Robeson begins his screen career with the lead in *Emperor Jones*; Roosevelt tries to end the Depression by raising farm prices; his program pays farmers not to raise as much food; tenant farmers lose their jobs and homes as a result, and the Depression goes on

Millions of Americans tune in to hear how Ma Perkins works out her problems on her new radio drama; Florence Price becomes the first African-American woman composer to have a piece performed by a major U.S. orchestra, the Chicago Symphony

On the West Coast, the Filipino Labor Union strikes for higher wages; farmers bring in other immigrant laborers and break the strike; income for Native Americans has fallen to an average of eighty-one dollars a year per person; Congress creates the Civil Works Administration to provide jobs during the hard winter of 1933-34; the program is so successful that it will be discontinued because some businessmen complain that it competes with private employers; the Public Works Administration is formed to create jobs on construction projects; it builds bridges, dams, schools, hospitals, city halls, and other public facilities but creates few jobs

1934 Start of the severe drought in regions of the Midwest and Great Plains — soon to be known as the Dust Bowl — drives many poor farmers off the land; many migrate to California looking for work picking crops, but there is not enough work for all those who need it; Filipino Labor Union

1935   strikes successfully against lettuce farmers for higher pay; June 1: African-Americans in Harlem boycott white merchants who do not hire black clerks; Hollywood movie makers, worried that Congress might censor their products, adopt the Production Code

1935   Congress passes the Repatriation Act, offering to pay Filipino-Americans to return to their homeland; in Harlem, rumors that an African-American boy was killed for shoplifting spark the Harlem riots against white-owned stores; actress Mae West earns the second-highest income in the country, $480,833; The Social Security Act passes Congress, providing help for the unemployed, elderly, sick, and disabled

1936   Union workers in Akron, Ohio, invent the sit-down strike in the first big CIO strike against manufacturers; Margaret Bourke-White and Erskine Caldwell publish *You Have Seen Their Faces*, a book about southern sharecropping; Walker Evans and James Agee live with Alabama tenant farm families to begin research for their book, *Let Us Now Praise Famous Men*

1938   The National Labor Relations Act protects the right of workers to form unions and bargain together with their employers; Congress passes the Fair Labor Standards Act, establishing minimum wages and maximum hours and outlawing child labor

1939   Congress ends the Federal Theater Project, whose productions were seen by over 25 million Americans in the four years it existed; *The Grapes of Wrath*, a novel by John Steinbeck about a tenant farm family made homeless by the Dust Bowl, is published and becomes a best-seller.

1941   December 7: The Japanese bomb Pearl Harbor in Hawaii; the U.S. enters World War II, during which more than four years of wartime spending will finally end the Great Depression

1945   April: Franklin D. Roosevelt dies in office during his fourth term as president

GLOSSARY

capital — material wealth, in the form of money or property, used or available for use in the production of more wealth by a person or business

depression — a very bad recession, or period when many of a country's resources are not being used to produce goods and services and many people are out of work

Dust Bowl — a name given to parts of the Midwest and Great Plains states during the terrible drought of the 1930s, when wind storms blew away much of the dry top soil in the region, taking with it the ability of tenant farmers to raise crops

Harlem Renaissance — a period in the 1920s when the Harlem community of New York City was the center of African-American culture; many musicians, actors, dancers, artists, and writers lived and worked in Harlem during this period, attracting European-American audiences to their performances and making lasting contributions to U.S. culture

Indian New Deal — a program largely unrelated to other New Deal programs, aimed at not only providing temporary emergency relief to American Indians but also reversing long-term U.S. policies that repressed Native cultures and addressing entrenched poverty among Native Americans

labor union — an organization of workers formed to represent their interests in bargaining with the owners or managers of business over working conditions or wages

migrant worker — a worker who travels from place to place taking temporary jobs, often on large farms,

	because no permanent work can be found or the worker lacks the qualifications for higher-paying, permanent work
New Deal	a phrase coined by Franklin Roosevelt, who promised a "new deal for the forgotten man"; the phrase was later applied both to government programs set up to fight the Depression and to the period in which they were enacted
Okies	people from Oklahoma, usually tenant farmers, who were forced off the land by drought and the Depression and often took to the road with all their possessions, looking for work
PWA	the Public Works Administration (PWA), created in 1933, which employed people by building bridges, dams, school buildings, hospitals, city buildings, and other public facilities
race movies	films produced in the early part of the twentieth century with African American casts and marketed to African American audiences
recession	a period when many of a country's resources are not being used to produce goods and services and many people are out of work
sharecropper	a tenant farmer whose rent was paid in the form of a large share of the crop raised by the farmer; sharecropping became common in the South after the Civil War, when freed African-Americans could not afford to buy their own land; poor white farmers also sometimes sharecropped; tenants were often exploited by landowners who charged them high interest rates on money borrowed to buy seed, supplies, and food until the crop could be harvested and sold
Social Security	a government program started during the Great Depression to give economic help to people who are unemployed, disabled, or elderly; both employers and employees are taxed to pay for Social Security
tenant farmer	a farmer who lived and raised crops on land rented from a landowner, either for cash or for a share of the crop raised
WPA	the Works Progress Administration, started in 1935, perhaps the biggest and most famous work relief program of the New Deal

FURTHER READING

Davies, Nancy M. *The Stock Market Crash of 1929.* New York: Macmillan Child Group (American Events Series), 1994.

Schraff, Anne. *The Great Depression and the New Deal: America's Economic Collapse and Recovery.* New York: Franklin Watts, 1990.

Speer, Bonnie. *Hillback to Boggy: A Family Struggles for Survival During the Great Depression, in a Tent in the Hills of Oklahoma.* As told by Jess Speer. Norman, Okla.: Reliance Press, 1992.

Stanley, Jerry. *Children of the Dustbowl: The True Story of the School at Weedpatch Camp.* New York: Crown Books, 1992.

Stewart, Gail B. *The New Deal.* New York: Macmillan Child Group (Timestop Books), 1993.

Terkel, Studs. *Hard Times: An Oral History of the Great Depression.* New York: Pantheon, 1970.

Woodburn, Judith. *A Multicultural Portrait of Labor in America.* New York: Marshall Cavendish, 1994.

Westin, Jean. *Making Do: How Women Survived the '30s.* Chicago: Follett, 1976.

Wormser, Richard L. *Growing Up in the Great Depression.* New York: Macmillan Child Group (Atheneum Child Books), 1993.

INDEX

African-Americans, 8, 10, 11, 14, 15, 16, 17, 18, 21, 28, 29, 31, 37, 41, 46, 48, 52, 54, 59, 60, 68, 71, 72, 73, 75
Agee, James, 20, 59
Agriculture, 37
Alabama, 20
All-girl dance orchestras, 17
American Federation of Labor (AFL), 63, 73, 74
American Indians, 19, 53, 65, 66
American Red Cross, 40
American Stock Exchange, 24
"Amos 'n' Andy," 10
Anderson, Eddie "Rochester," 15
Anderson, Ivie, 6
Arkansas, 40, 50
Armstrong, Louis, 18
Art, 7, 19, 20
Asian-Americans, 52. *See also* individual Asian-American groups
Astaire, Fred, 13
Atlanta, 68
Aunt Sammy, 39

Bank holidays, 27
Banks, 27, 57; and "runs" on, 27; and rioting, 51
Beavers, Hattie, 16
Bellow, Saul, 18
Benny, Jack, 15
Bethune, Mary McLeod, 48
Betty Crocker, 39
Black Thursday, 22, 23, 25
Books, 7
Bourke-White, Margaret, 20
Boycotts, 72
Bridge, 12
Britain (British), 15
Broadway, 15, 19
Brokerage firms, 24, 25
Buck, Pearl, 21
Businesses, 24, 29
Buying "on margin," 24

Caldwell, Erskine, 20
California, 49, 55, 58, 62, 63, 69
Canning food, 39
Capra, Frank, 13
Cheever, John, 18
Chicago Symphony, 17
Chicago, 19, 31, 51, 68
Child labor laws, 28

Children, 47, 48, 49, 50, 52, 53, 57; and dropping out of school, 32, 33, 48, 49; and growing up early, 32, 47; and homelessness of, 33
Chinatown, 52
Chinese-Americans, 52
Christian evangelists, 10
Civil War, 28, 59
Civil Works Administration (CWA), 32, 67
Civilian Conservation Corps (CCC), 52, 60, 65; and discrimination against women, 60
Clothing, 36; and shortage of, 48, 54
College, 51, 52
Communism, 11, 19, 29, 73
Congress of Industrial Organizations (CIO), 74
Correll, Charles, 10
Cotton Club, 18
Coughlin, Charles ("Radio Priest"), 10, 11; and anti-Semitism, 10
Crash, the, 23, 25, 26
Crawford, Joan, 13, 14
Culture, 7

Dance, 7, 16, 17, 18
Davis, Bette, 13
Davis, Maxine, 51
De Kooning, Willem, 19
Defense industry, 45
Democratic Party, 28, 29, 75
Detroit, 31, 64
Disabilities, 8, 11
Division of Negro Affairs, 48
Divorce, 40
Drought, 48
Dust Bowl, 13, 49, 55, 61, 62

East Indians (Asians), 63
Economy, 23, 24, 25
Education, 42, 60
Ellington, Edward Kennedy "Duke", 6, 17, 18
Ellison, Ralph, 18
Europe (Europeans), 20, 57
European-Americans, 16, 63; and racism, 68
Evans, Walker, 20, 59

Fascism, 11
Factory work, 70, 72
Fair Labor Standards Act, 74

Family life, 33, 34, 38, 39, 40, 42, 45, 54, 64, 69; and traditional roles, 33, 35, 45
Farming, 8, 9, 44, 47, 48, 49, 50, 57, 58, 62, 63, 66, 70, 73, 74; African-Americans, 59; Japanese, 63; Mexicans, 63; tenant, 7, 31, 44, 49, 58, 60, 61, 62
Federal Art Project, 19
Federal Department of Labor, 72
Federal insurance for banks, 28
Federal Music Project, 20; and discrimination against women, 20
Federal Theater Project, 19, 20
Federal Writers Project (FWP), 18, 19
Female vocalists, 6
Fetchit, Stepin, 15
Fields, W. C., 15
Filipino Labor Union (FLU), 63
Film, 7, 12, and battle-of-the-sexes themes, 14; and gangsters, 12; and idols, 16; and reinforcement of stereotypes, 14, 15, 16; and roles for women, 13, 14; and sex, 14; as an escape, 13; documentaries, 20; gangster movies, 13; musicals, 13; race, 16, 17
Fireside chats, 9, 28
Fitzgerald, Ella, 18
Florida Writers Project, 21
Florida, 26
Ford, John, 13
Foreclosures, 57
Forty-hour work week, 28, 74

Galbraith, John Kenneth, 25
Gellhorn, Martha, 20
General Mills, 39
Georgia, 46, 68
Germany (Germans), 11
Godsen, Freeman, 10
Golden Gate Bridge, 69
Government projects, 69
Government, and changing role of, 28
Grandma Moses. *See* Anna Mary Robertson
Great Plains, 48, 49, 55, 61, 62

Great War. *See* World War I
Gypsies, 11

"Hardluck Town," 30
Harlem Renaissance, 17, 21, 71
Harlem, 18, 71, 72
Hawaii, 63, 74
Henderson, Fletcher, 18
Hepburn, Katherine, 13
High school, 51
Hitler, Adolf, 11
Hoboes, 8, 40, 53, 54, 55
Holiday, Billie, 18
Hollywood, 12, 14, 15
Home economists, 38, 39
Homeless shelters, 53
Homelessness, 31, 36, 53, 54
Homosexuality, 11
Hoover, Herbert, 9, 29
Hurston, Zora Neale, 18

Illinois, 27
Immigrants, 8, 63, 64
India (Indians), 64
Indian Emergency Conservation Camp, 66
Indian emergency conservation program, 53
Indian New Deal, 65
Ink Spots, 18
Iowa, 9
Italy (Italians), 11

Jackson, Mahalia, 18
Japan (Japanese), 63
Japan (Japanese), 74
Japanese-Americans, 52
Jell-O, 39
Judaism, 11

Kansas City, 18
Kansas, 61
Kansas, 70

Labor unions, 73
Lange, Dorothea, 59
Latinos, 37, 41, 42
Law of supply and demand, 26
Laws of economics, 26
Lincoln, Abraham, 28
Lincoln, Abraham, 75
Literature, 18
Little Rascals, the, 13
"Living newspapers," 19
London, 15
Los Angeles, 64

Los Angeles Women's Symphony, 17

Ma Perkins. See Payne, Virginia
Manhattan, 64
Marriage, 40
McCullers, Carson, 21
McDaniel, Hattie, 15, 16
Men: and pressure, 42; and social expectations, 41; and suicide, 40, 41, 43; and traditional roles, 41; and violence, 40; traditional roles of, 38
Mexican Bureau, 64
Mexican immigrants, 8, 48, 64
Mexican-Americans, 8, 48, 64; and deportation, 8; farmers, 8
Mexico (Mexicans), 49, 62, 63, 65, 73
Mexico City, 64
Micheaux, Oscar, 16
Michigan, 48
Migrant workers, 42, 44, 48, 49, 53, 55, 64; and labor camps, 49, 63
Mills Brothers, 18
Minehan, Tom, 54
Miniature golf, 7
Minimum wage, 28, 74
Minorities, 8, 35, 41, 52, 60; and discrimination against, 25, 31; and slaughter of in Europe, 11
Missionaries, 54
Missions, 53, 54
Missouri, 44, 51
Music, 7, 10, 16, 17, 18; and African-Americans, 10, 18; and big bands, 16; and discrimination, 17; blues, 9, 17, 18; classical, 17, 20; folk, 20; gospel, 9, 17, 18; jazz, 6, 9, 16, 17, 18; swing, 16, 18
Musical instruments, 6
Mussolini, Benito, 11

National League for Decency, the, 14
National Youth Administration (NYA), 48, 52
Native Americans. See American Indians
Native Sons and Daughters of the Golden West, 52
Nazism, 11
New Deal, 18, 19, 28, 37, 48, 52, 60, 63, 74, 75
New England, 58
New Jersey, 42
New York, 17, 27, 56, 68
New York City, 24, 25, 30, 41, 71
New York Stock Exchange, 22, 23, 24
New York World's Fair, 19
Newspaper ads: and discrimination, 68, 69

O'Keefe, Georgia, 21
"Okies," 49
O'Neill, Eugene, 15
Oklahoma City, 54
Oklahoma, 49, 61
Olsen, Tillie, 18
Oregon, 65, 66
Oregon American Indians, 53

Painting, 7, 18
Panic, 26, 27, 31
Payne, Virginia, 11, 12
Pearl Harbor, 74
Perkins, Frances, 69, 70
Philippines (Filipinos), 8, 49, 63, 73; and discrimination against, 63, 64; as cheap labor, 63
Photographs, 7
Picketing, 32
Pinoys. See Philippines (Filipinos), 63
Pittsburgh, 8
Plantations, 59, 63
Planters. See plantation owners
Poland (Poles), 11
Polio, 8
Pollack, Jackson, 19
Popular culture, 7, 8
Porter, Katherine Anne, 21
Poverty, 39, 42, 59, 64, 66
Production Code, 14
Property, 68

Public assistance, 28
Public Welfare Department, 64
Public Works Administration (PWA), 67

"Radical journalism," 20
Radio Priest. See Coughlin, Charles
Radio, 7, 9, 10, 12, 39, 40; and personalities, 11; and religious programs, 10; as a lasting symbol of life in the thirties, 9; as a powerful medium, 9, 11; as free entertainment, 10
Realism, 7
Recession, 25, 26
Recording companies, 7, 10
Redman, Don, 18
Relief programs, 65
Repatriation Act, 63, 64
Republican Party, 28, 75
Reservation lands, 65
Robertson, Anna Mary "Grandma" Moses, 21
Robeson, Paul, 15
Robinson, Bill "Bojangles," 13, 15
Rogers, Ginger, 13
Roosevelt, Eleanor (Anna), 8, 43, 48; as conscience of the nation, 29
Roosevelt, Franklin Delano, 8, 9, 10, 18, 19, 27, 28, 29, 58, 60, 61, 65, 67, 78
Roosevelt, Theodore, 8, 29
Russell, Rosalind, 13

San Antonio, 37
San Francisco, 69
San Joaquin Valley, 55
Sarton, May, 21
Savannah, 46
School lunch program, 50
School, 50, 53, 65
Sculpture, 18
Segregation, 71; at movie theaters, 7, 14, 15; in the music industry, 17
Sharecropping, 20, 34, 44, 45, 59, 60, 61
Social programs, 36

Social Security, 28, 37, 74
Socialism, 11, 29
Songs, 7
Soup kitchens, 53
Speculating, 24
Squatters, 30, 45
Steinbeck, John, 13, 39, 59
Stocks, 24, 27
Strikes, 20, 21, 74
Sugar beet fields, 48
Supreme Court, 73

Television, 9, 12
Temple, Shirley, 13, 14, 15
Texas, 48, 61, 62
Theater, 18

U.S. Congress, 8, 14, 19, 20, 73, 74
U.S. Navy, 8
Uncle Sam, 39
Unemployment, 8, 34, 39, 41, 42, 43, 44, 66, 68, 69, 75; and emotional impact for men, 43
United Nations, 29
Unskilled jobs, 68, 73
Vagrancy laws, 54
Vagrants. See Homelessness
Valentino, Rudolph, 16

Walker, Margaret, 18
Wall Street, 22, 24, 26, 27
Waller, Fats, 18
Warm Springs Reservation, 65
West, Mae, 14, 16
Westin, Jean, 54
Wilson, Woodrow, 8
Women, 17, 37, 40, 41, 42, 43, 69, 70, 73; and discrimination against, 25, 31, 68; and roles on farms, 35, 37; and traditional roles, 37, 38, 39, 40, 42; and working outside the home, 36, 37
Work programs, 67
Working conditions, 72, 73
Works Progress Administration (WPA), 67
World War I, 25, 51, 57
World War II, 7, 8, 20, 23, 45, 63, 74
Wright, Richard, 18